The Art of Creative Nonfiction

Wiley Books for Writers Series

Book Editors Talk to Writers, by Judy Mandell

Magazine Editors Talk to Writers, by Judy Mandell

Networking at Writers Conferences: From Contacts to Contracts, by Steven D. Spratt and Lee G. Spratt

The Elements of Storytelling: How to Write Compelling Fiction, by Peter Rubie

The Complete Guide to Writers Groups, Conferences, and Workshops, by Eileen Malone

The Art of Creative Nonfiction

Writing and Selling the Literature of Reality

Lee Gutkind

John Wiley & Sons, Inc.

New York • Chichester • Brisbane • Toronto• Singapore• Weinheim

Copyright © 1997 by Lee Gutkind.

Library of Congress Cataloging-in-Publication Data

Gutkind, Lee.
    The art of creative non-fiction :   writing and selling the
literature of reality   /   Lee Gutkind.
        p.   cm.–(Wiley books for writers series)
    ISBN 0-471-11356-5
    1. Authorship.   I. Title.   II. Series.
PN145.G86   1997
808'.02–dc20   96-28002
                                                       CIP

Printed in the United States of America

10 9 8 7 6 5 4 3 2 1

Contents

Introduction

Writing for the Reader

This book, *The Art of Creative Nonfiction: Writing and Selling the Literature of Reality*, will introduce the genre of creative nonfiction and explain it with meticulousness—from idea through structure and development to finished product.

The organization of *The Art of Creative Nonfiction: Writing and Selling the Literature of Reality* respects the order shown in the name of the genre. Part I confronts creative matters: It presents the anatomy of the essay by breaking down the essay, article, and book into their vital components and analyzing the creative structure so that readers understand how to design and build a provocative creative nonfiction effort.

Part II is the nonfiction part, dealing with a writer's search for a salable subject for books, articles, and essays, and the unique challenge of gathering and communicating information from a personal point of view and the intimate process writers often call immersion.

Among other things in this book, you will learn a great deal about the writing life. You will see how long it takes to write a book, essay, or article, how hard a writer must work, how diligently he or she must research, read, and fact check—and the skill involved in revealing a subject with qualities that contain universal appeal, because the true test of a creative nonfiction writer is to attract and capture readers who do not have a built-in fascination or connection to a subject or narrator.

One of the most memorable compliments I ever received through an eight-book, 25-year career as an author, essayist, teacher, and editor is from a woman who began idly leafing through her husband's copy of my book about National League baseball umpires called *The Best Seat in Baseball, But You Have to Stand*:

"I have always hated baseball. It's a boring game. When my husband and son are watching it on TV, I leave the house. But I realized, as I looked through your book, that these were real people with unique problems—not just baseball fanatics—you were writing about. I sat down and read the book cover to cover in two nights."

This is the basic objective of creative nonfiction: Capturing and describing a subject so that the most resistant reader will be interested in learning more about it. The writer establishes a certain humanistic expertise, becoming a reader's filter so that the reader will gain intellectual substance (about baseball, politics, science, or any other subject) while focusing on the drama and intensity of ordinary people living unusual, stressful, and compelling lives.

Part 1

The Creative Part

For Writers, Thinkers, Silent Observers (and Other People with Stories to Tell)

1.1 Crossing Genres

Today there are just as many poets, playwrights, and fiction writers writing creative nonfiction as there are journalists—perhaps more.

Novelists John Updike and Louise Erdrich, poets Diane Ackerman and Adrienne Rich have recently published collections of essays and memoirs, a very popular form of creative nonfiction. Essays by poets, novelists, and playwrights are appearing with increasing frequency not only in literary journals, but also in popular magazines and newspapers. Says poet Donald Morrill, "All the years I have been working on poetry (learning metaphorical structures, rhythm, imagery) have made me a better prose writer."

1.2 Thinkers and Scholars—Reaching Out from Academia

Creative nonfiction demands spontaneity and an imaginative approach, while remaining true to the validity and integrity of the information it contains. That is why the creative nonfiction form is so appealing to people with new ideas or fresh interpretations of accepted concepts in history, science, or the arts; people with an intellectual curiosity about the world around us or a fresh viewpoint or approach to staid and seemingly inaccessible disciplines.

For example: the Harvard University anthropologist Stephen Jay Gould, whose essays often explain principles of evolution and geology through discussions of the origin of baseball or cable car rides in San Francisco. Or Lewis Thomas or Oliver Sacks, whose perspectives on science in general and neurology in particular have provided a general reading audience with special insight.

Biographies are often considered to be works of creative nonfiction. David McCullough, winner of the Pulitzer Prize and the National Book Award, has written accurately and creatively about Harry Truman, Theodore Roosevelt, and the Brooklyn Bridge. An increasing number of historians, including Simon Schama (*The Landscapes of My Life*), are creative nonfiction writers, although they call themselves or are described by others as "narrative historians."

1.3 And People with Stories to Tell

Autobiographies—memoirs—are becoming increasingly popular, as shown by recent record-setting bestsellers by Colin Powell, Jimmy Carter, Donald Trump, and Gore Vidal. Or the many tell-it-all books about O.J. and Nicole Simpson, the sex life of Bill Clinton, and the tragic and frightening story of the Menendez brothers. Not to forget books by Oprah Winfrey, Michael Jordan, and Charleton Heston—there are celebrities ad infinitum. These authors may not be considered "scholars" or thinkers but many may have compelling stories to tell, and stories, after all, are what good literature of any genre is all about.

1.4 Flies on the Wall

The books and essays of Gould, Thomas, and Sacks provide windows through which the general public can observe situations that are often inaccessible. In a recent book, Oliver Sacks writes about learning of a surgeon who had Tourette's Syndrome—a malady that would seem to render surgery impossible. Sacks decided to spend a week living in the surgeon's home with the doctor and his family. He accompanies the surgeon into the operating room and into the sky (the surgeon is a private pilot) and then Sacks shares the intimate perspective he has gained of this unique man with his readers.

Sacks is a neurologist, and so his curiosity about the surgeon with Tourette's is related to his profession, but the vast majority of creative nonfiction writers have little official connection to the subjects about which they choose to write.

Tracy Kidder has become a fly on the wall with construction companies (*House*) and elementary schools (*Among School Children*). Gay Talese (*Honor Thy Father*), John McPhee (*Coming Into the Country*), George Plimpton (*Paper Lion*), and Diane Ackerman (*Natural History of the Senses*) are well-known writers whose successful careers have been founded on taking advantage of opportunities for adventure.

I have spent years as a writer and watcher, wandering the country on a motorcycle in order to learn about the motorcycle subculture, laboring as a wrangler on a rodeo, scrubbing with heart and liver transplant surgeons, traveling with a crew of National League baseball umpires, performing as a clown for Ringling Brothers Circus, observing behind the scenes at a children's hospital, working with zoo veterinarians—all research for books, essays, and articles.

1.5   Terminology

In this book, the words *essay* and *article* are used interchangeably. Essentially, essays and articles are very similar, although essay is used more often when the prose piece being written is more personal—when it is your own thoughts—than objective, formulaic, or verifiable, as in articles. An in-depth article or essay that concentrates on a place or a person is called a profile.

When I refer to creative nonfiction books I include memoirs (or autobiography), and documentary drama (a term more often used to refer to films, such as *Hoop Dreams*, which captures the lives of two inner-city high school basketball players over a six-year period).

Much of what is generically referred to as literary journalism can be classified as creative nonfiction. In the early 1960s, author and social commentator Tom Wolfe (*The Right Stuff, The Electric Kool Aid Acid Test*) coined a term that lasted for more than a decade—the "new journalism."

Wolfe's new journalism faded, but over the past five years creative nonfiction clearly has evolved as the accepted way of describing what is becoming the most important and popular genre in the literary world today.

The best magazines—*The New Yorker, Harper's, Vanity Fair, Esquire*—publish more creative nonfiction than fiction and poetry combined. Universities offer Master's of Fine Arts degrees in creative nonfiction. A rapidly increasing number of books are in the creative nonfiction form.

Newspapers are publishing an increasing amount of creative nonfiction, not only as features but on news and op-ed pages as well. Former *New York Times* columnist Anna Quindlen writes creative nonfiction, as does her successor, Maureen Dowd, whose stories often appear on the front page.

You will learn to distinguish accurately between traditional nonfiction, journalism, and creative nonfiction as the book evolves.

1.6   A Passion for People

What does it take to be a good creative nonfiction writer?

Usually, when people are discussing essays, articles, or nonfiction books, they use words such as *interesting, accurate*, perhaps even *fascinating. Passion* and *intimacy* are not words that are often attached to nonfiction; they sound too spontaneous, emotional, and imprecise.

But passion is what is required of a creative nonfiction writer if he or she is to be successful: A passion for the written word; a passion for the search and discovery of knowledge; and a passion for involvement—observing both directly and clandestinely in order to understand intimately how things in this world work.

A Definition of the Genre—The Boundaries of the Profession

2.1   *The Truth in Fiction*

People ask, "Creative nonfiction sounds like a contradiction in terms. How can you be creative if you are writing nonfiction? After all, isn't fiction mostly made up or imagined stories, and isn't nonfiction necessarily real and true?" The answers to those questions, although they seem to be obvious on the surface, are as clear as mud.

For example, fiction is not completely untrue. *The Bridges of Madison County*, about which Robert James Waller writes in his best-selling novel, do in fact exist, as does Madison County, Iowa, where the story takes place. But even if Madison County was fictitious, the details about the place must ring true in readers' minds. Otherwise, the book would not be believable.

Some of the most fantastic novels, such as those by Stephen King, are framed with accurate locations and familiar characters. King's stories have been compelling and terrifying because they are believable. If readers did not accept the locations, the characters, and even the basic plot outline, then Stephen King would not be the household name he is today.

Conversely, some movies—or novels—are *nearly* true. The films *Apollo 13* with Tom Hanks and *This Boy's Life* with Robert DeNiro, both adapted from nonfiction books, are good examples of fact enhanced by fiction. *Jaws*, which terrified and delighted a generation of readers and viewers in the 1970s, continues to strike a familiar and frightening chord when rerun on TV, usually in the early summers when the beaches are about to open.

Thus, the closer to the truth fiction is, the closer to what might be perceived as possible, the more it will impact upon a reading audience. And the more that writing affects readers, the more popular it will become. It is an unyielding circle. To touch and affect readers, fiction must ring true. Nonfiction, conversely, must not only ring true, it must *be* true.

2.2 A Different Level of Truth in Creative Nonfiction

Before I launch into a discussion of the nature of truth, let me qualify the above remark: Traditional journalists learn early in their education that creativity or imagination in newspapers and magazines are basically disallowed. Reporters with any real literary talent will have it squeezed out of them by stubborn and insensitive editors. Disillusioned, they will write secretly at night (becoming closet poets or novelists), or they leave the profession to chase their muse or some other dream.

This is what is so uplifting and satisfying about creative nonfiction: You can be a reporter and a *writer*, too.

Reporters are told that "truth" means, among other things, that their work must be accurate and informational. Nothing concerning the people, places, and situations about which they are writing can be altered or made up. This paean to information and accuracy should reverberate in the mind of the creative nonfiction writer as well.

Information is the goal of the nonfiction writer—teaching or enlightening a reader is the unalterable mission of all nonfiction. The importance of providing accurate information cannot be overemphasized: Names, dates, places, descriptions, quotations may not be created or altered for any reason, at any time.

In this regard, creative nonfiction is as accurate as the most meticulous reportage—perhaps even more accurate because the creative nonfiction writer is expected to dig deeper into a subject, thereby presenting or unearthing a larger truth. The Pulitzer Prize-winning coverage of the Watergate affair by Bob Woodward and Carl Bernstein is a prime example of the larger truth that it is possible to achieve in creative nonfiction.

The hard facts of the Watergate scandal, which toppled Richard Nixon's presidency, were reported in an explosive series of stories over a period of weeks by Woodward and Bernstein in the *Washington Post*. But anyone who has read the book (*All The President's Men*) or seen the film based on the book (another example of nonfiction that is fictionalized to enhance dramatic impact) will be presented with a much more complete and well-rounded story. The characters are described with three-dimensional perspective and the intricacies and conflicts inherent in the story are analyzed and debated. All of this is missing from the *Washington Post's* account.

Also missing in the newspaper account are the challenges and adventures of Woodward and Bernstein themselves as they investigate the Watergate break-in and begin to pierce the armor of the White House cover-up—the writers' personal stories behind the news stories. This truth is also part of the larger truth—the story behind the storytellers. It is the most exciting and revealing aspect of the story and would have never been included in a traditional journalistic version.

Not only must it be scrupulously accurate, the traditional reporter is told, reportage must be balanced. That means that when possible, an equal amount of positive and negative information about the subject must be included to make the story fair to everyone involved.

In creative nonfiction, balance and objectivity are certainly permitted and sometimes desirable. But they are not requirements. On the contrary.

2.3   Objectivity and Subjectivity

Truth to the traditional reporter encompasses objectivity, meaning that the reporter must not allow personal feelings to enter into the writing of the story. Like Jack Webb in the old and often rerun *Dragnet* TV series, they are seeking "Just the facts, ma'am." What the reporter/

writer feels or thinks personally about the nature or truth of the story is irrelevant. Curiously, most everyone in the newspaper business will admit that objectivity is impossible, but that doesn't seem to diminish the intensity of their belief in the principle.

More often than not, writers turn to the creative nonfiction genre because they feel passionately about a person, place, subject, or issue and have no interest in or intention of maintaining a balanced or objective tone or viewpoint. Writers turn to creative nonfiction because they have a true story to tell, often involving themselves, and they do not want to be reined in or controlled by Big Brother rules and regulations.

Subjectivity should not be confused with editorializing, however. Readers interested in personal opinion and advocacy journalism will read the op-ed pages of newspapers and magazines. They will buy books by people who are known to be passionate and opinionated experts in their own field—from Dr. Kevorkian to evangelist Billy Graham. Conceivably, writers with a mission can write creative nonfiction, but only if they are able to illustrate—with accuracy—the particular viewpoint that they are advocating.

A good example of advocacy nonfiction, "Guilt by Provocation" is written for a newspaper audience, but it contains all the elements of good creative nonfiction, including a personal voice, a subjective point of view, and a definite story and scene, all designed to reach out and embrace a reader. "The Incident," the first chapter of my book, *Stuck in Time, The Tragedy of Childhood Mental Illness* (Readings section), is a second example, but it is much more dramatic and experiential and probably would never be published in a newspaper. However, the stories are similar in many ways.

"Guilt by Provocation"
ELIZABETH BOLTSON GORDON*

A long time ago, I learned a lesson about the power of words.

*Reprinted by permission of the author.

Thus, I found myself that July, more than 30 years ago, as one of four counselors in a cabin with 20 boys who were around 8 years old—and who most desperately needed male mentoring that girl counselors could not provide. I was well-intentioned, but young, with no training or guidance—naive about the problems of my campers, especially those of the tougher inner-city kids.

One day, another counselor and I were disciplining a youngster named Tommy. I had found this kid frightening ever since I had overheard him graphically describe some horrifying things he had done to a younger sister. The other counselor, nicknamed Skipper, was a plain, stocky girl who acted tough and tended to bully the kids. I remember the two of us inside the cabin, backing Tommy against the wall to get him to admit to some wrongdoing.

Uncomfortable with the situation, I imitated Skipper's aggressive stance. We thrust our faces into his, trying to be as menacing as possible. Skipper emphasized her gestures with the brightly colored lanyard she held in her hand. Tommy, not easily intimidated, continued to defy us. Casting about for a way to break the impasse, I came up with a new tactic. I leaned in even closer and began to threaten him: "If you don't tell us, we'll hit you."

The browbeating went on for a while, with no response. And then—Skipper hit Tommy across the face with the lanyard.

I was stunned. None of us had ever hit a kid before. I knew that it was very wrong and that more violence was the last thing Tommy needed. I remember thinking, "I never meant to hit him. I thought it was understood that we were only trying to frighten him."

I knew I was responsible. I had egged Skipper on. Indeed, I had put the idea in her head. I had assumed that we both understood that we were bluffing. She, justifiably, felt that she was acting with my approval. I felt awful. I knew that I had set in motion the chain of events that had led to the unthinkable.

My memory ends with Tommy's being struck, and my own remorse. I don't recall whether or not he eventually caved in.

I had learned a lesson then that I have never forgotten. It's a variation on the well-known aphorism about being careful what you wish for. It goes something like: "Be careful what you say. Someone might act as if you mean it."

All it takes is someone closer to the edge, perhaps a bit more unbalanced or extreme than you are, or someone who simply takes you at your word, who doesn't share your understanding that there's a line that isn't to be crossed no matter how heated the rhetoric.

The line is then crossed, and the one who put the idea there at the outset must face his or her culpability.

I was recently reminded of the incident with Tommy as I thought about Binyamin Netanyahu, the leader of Israel's opposition Likud Party, and his response to the murder of Yitzhak Rabin.

Bibi, as he is called, had allowed his followers to depict Rabin in recent months as a traitor to Israel, a murderer, even a Nazi. Accepting this view of Rabin would make his demise justifiable, desirable, even necessary. It made him fair game.

After the assassination, Bibi worked hard at distancing himself from the act and its perpetrator. He woke up one day after the assassination, he tells us, "with a shudder running through his whole body."

I recognize that shudder. I too have felt it—every time I think about Tommy and see Skipper whip that lanyard across his face.

2.4   Reorienting the Writer's Eye

To begin thinking in the creative nonfiction mode you must begin to reorient your writing eye.

Study the articles and essays in the Readings section in the back of this book. Picture the author. Concentrate on understanding the writer's place or position in the narrative—where he or she fits—and how the information presented in the essay was actually gathered.

Go to newsstands and leaf through magazines, searching for the writer in each nonfiction narrative. Try to picture yourself in those stories.

What would you do to gather information and create drama—simultaneously? Begin a list of essays and articles you would like to write that involve a writer as both actor and observer.

Let us say that you have an interest in writing about life in a local police station. How will you make yourself a part of the place without being obtrusive?

Or perhaps you want to write about aspects of your family—a daughter's inability to get along with her mother or a son with a father. Where will you and your own parents fit into the research-writing equation? How will you make it personal and at the same time universal in appeal?

Begin planning for your life as a creative nonfiction writer. Start work now by remembering your mission:

Creative nonfiction differs from fiction because it is necessarily and scrupulously accurate and the presentation of information, a teaching element to readers, is paramount. Creative nonfiction differs from traditional reportage, however, because balance is unnecessary and subjectivity is not only permitted but encouraged.

3

The Devices of Creative Nonfiction

3.1 Description

The term *literary license* is often used in reference to writers who manipulate truth and accuracy in stories—what really happened—to enhance dramatic impact and, therefore, to make a story more readable or exciting.

Creative nonfiction writers, however, are permitted a different form of literary license: to use the literary devices previously and exclusively available to the fiction writer (and the poet and playwright) in the writing of their true and accurate creative nonfiction stories. In other words, nonfiction writers cannot alter the facts, but they can capture and present them much more dramatically.

What are these literary devices to which I refer? Think about some of the novels mentioned in this book so far, such as *The Bridges of Madison County* or *Jaws*. Or stroll through the stacks of your public library for favorite titles; browse your neighborhood bookstore for the newest and hottest best-sellers.

What do you remember enjoying about the books and stories you liked best? What literary or writing techniques are evident? There is a great deal of dramatic description of people and places (and even feelings) in the best novels, short stories, and essays, for one thing. Who will ever forget the massive and overwhelming onslaught of the whales in *Moby Dick* or the bloody endless battles in *The Red Badge of Courage?* Observing and recording such dramatic description is a hallmark of creative nonfiction prose.

Here is a description of an event, startling to an unaware reader, but an everyday occurrence in the life of a farm veterinarian named Wendy Freeman, from my essay "Difficult Decisions," published in the literary journal *Prairie Schooner* in the Fall 1966 issue. It offers a vivid and memorable window of reality to readers—a license more often employed in fiction.

Freeman locates a spot in the barn directly beside an electric outlet and plugs in the dis-budding iron. She walks outside, opens a pen in which two calves are waiting, selects a brown spotted calf ("The kind that makes chocolate milk," she jokes) and brings it inside. Working quickly, she shaves the hair from around the horns, then reaches into her medicine bag for Lidocaine, a pain blocker, which she has already siphoned into a hypodermic needle. She injects the Lidocaine into the calf's head directly around the horn.

Next comes the electric dis-budding iron, which resembles a branding iron, round, like a large "O," not unlike a packaged donut with a hole in the middle. She grabs the calf's ear, wedges its head against her body, inserts the "O" of the iron through the calf's horn, and then, bringing the iron slowly downward, digs the hot iron into the calf's little head.

First there is a whiff of bluish white smoke, and then the dank, stark stench of burning fur. Then comes the richer more primeval aroma of roasting skin, followed by the sound of searing bone, as she applies increasing pressure. She twists the iron back and forth repeatedly until smoking copper colored rings show through above the ears. It looks as if the smoke is emanating from the calf's head, as if the soul of this tiny helpless animal has suddenly been apprehended by the devil.

Another example from my book *Bike Fever*, this time from the rain-soaked seat of a motorcycle, is excerpted below. As you read, remember that these incidents are true and quite common, but they are rendered to the reader in the dramatic and descriptive manner of the fiction writer setting a scene and embellishing an event.

"Days and Nights: Heading South"

Air leaked into my rainsuit and inflated me. The rainsuit collar flapped fast in the wind, plastic against plastic, sounding like the propeller of a small airplane. After a while, the rainsuit ripped from the force of the wind, and water soaked the jacket under it. The weight of the wet jacket was heavy on my shoulders. The wetness stuck to my warm skin and I shivered as I rode. Periodically, I wiped water from my face shield, drenching my gloves. The water rolling from the gauntlets of my gloves swept under the shield and soaked my face. My cheeks started to itch and I scratched them with my wet gloves. The rain, blown by the wind, pricked my chin and rolled down my neck. Cold water puddled on the seat, shriveling my crotch. Trucks coming in the opposite direction punched me with mud, while my tires skidded over the pavement on water mixed with oil leaked from hot engines. The brake linings got wet and grabbed dangerously. The water, rolling off the seat, drained down my leg, filling my boot.

Burt and I were riding our motorcycles on Skyline Drive near Staunton, Virginia, and it had been raining for eight straight days.

Three hours out of Pittsburgh, the rain had started. We detoured south into Cumberland, Maryland, then into West Virginia, but the rain kept up. We went northeast back into Pennsylvania, then south into West Virginia and Virginia, but the water dogged us. We stopped at taverns and diners along the way for television weather reports, then headed toward the warm fronts, looking for a dry pocket in which to rest. During the day, rain soaked our gear. We couldn't cook at night. We bought plastic garbage bags to cover everything, but when the wind was strong, it ripped the plastic. Every morning we first found a town with a laundromat, and for twenty-five cents, bought some man-made sun.

On the eighth day, the fog came up in the Shenandoah Mountains. We traveled the whole day through fog that stuck in our eyes and wafted over the road. We followed the road by watching the shapes of the trees that lined the edge of the pavement. I could see the wheels on my motorcycle as we crept through the mountains, but not where they touched the ground. I could see the glowing eyes of cars coming in the opposite direction, but never the exact shapes of the cars or the people inside. Sometimes I could see Burt's red taillight in front of me and sometimes I couldn't. It was the thickest fog I have ever seen. Creeping through it the whole day, we could make only fifty miles.

I have never been skydiving, but driving through that fog is how I would imagine it. We floated through the clouds, guided by the way the wheels sounded against the road; we could tell when we neared the edge of the road, because some of the pebbles spilling from the shoulder, swept up by the tires, would clink against our exhaust pipes.

And we relied on our memories of riding in the past. If you think back hard enough to a special day, when the sun was warm and you cruised a long mountain road, if you can remember how it was and can concentrate, then you can duplicate that ride even though you cannot see. Taking the turns just as you have so many times before, leaning just enough, straightening slowly, feeling for the right balance, rolling that way. You don't always need eyes to ride a motorcycle, as long as you have a good memory and the ability to recreate what you know you should see.

The persistence of the rain dulls your perceptions, but

the fog reactivates them. You can taste the rain in the fog. And since you cannot see trees, grass, and wildflowers, you smell them. There are actually lines in the fog; it is not just a milky haze; streams of fog of different shades come together to make a screen. It feels strangely warm against your face, slightly wet. You push away the fog with your hand and, like water, more flows in to take its place. Floating through the fog seems both prehistoric and futuristic; it is in that gap where earth loses contact with the heavens.

3.2   Dialogue: Characters Who Communicate

Another technique fiction writers employ to enhance reality and establish action is dialogue. In stories from the old masters, such as Ernest Hemingway and John Steinbeck, or the new masters, such as Raymond Carver and Joyce Carol Oates, people talk to one another endlessly, page after page, as in real life.

Traditional reporters will paraphrase the subjects they are interviewing and provide short sound bites within quotation marks to instill a sense of reality and authenticity, but in real life—and in creative nonfiction (often called the literature of reality)—people communicate with spoken words. Writers report or recreate entire conversations as in this scene from my upcoming book, called *An Unspoken Art: Profiles of Veterinary Life*:

After going through his getting-acquainted kissing dance with a pudgy brown springer spaniel suffering from chronic diarrhea, veterinarian Gene Solomon asks the heavyset, well-dressed woman, accompanied by her teenage daughter, "Tell me what you feed her."

The woman gulps and lowers her head.

"Yes, tell him, Mother," the daughter says.

"Chicken."

"Chicken," Solomon nods calmly and writes something into the dog's chart. "Anything else?"

Once again, the woman gulps, as if she's been caught in an act that she had been trying to conceal, which, of course, is absolutely true. "Fruit," she says.

"Fruit?"

"Yes, raisins, bananas . . ."

"And kiwi," her daughter adds.

Solomon nods again, writes in the chart and carefully eyeballs the patient. The woman's daughter is now smiling widely, on the verge of laughter.

"Any normal food?" Solomon asks. He is straightforward and matter of fact. He does not make any attempt to call attention to this odd dietary regimen. "I mean, normal dog food?" he corrected himself.

Again the woman swallows. "Well . . . bagels," she says.

"Well," says Solomon calmly, "bagels are better than fruit and chicken, but if you intend to continue to feed her chicken then take the skin off—and eliminate the dark meat."

"But she likes dark meat."

Solomon shrugs. "White meat only is best for your dog in the chicken category."

"She really prefers dark meat," the woman repeats.

"Well," says Solomon, "If she's that picky . . ."

"Okay, okay," says the woman, "I guess I can do that."

Now the daughter bursts out laughing. Solomon, however, remains calm and deadpan, regarding the situation with a professional distance, while continuing to pet and kiss the brown little dog with the floppy ears. The mother, who has been growing increasingly uncomfortable, is now blushing; she has moved far back into the corner of the examination room. She sinks down to the ground, covering her face with her hands. "What's wrong with you, Mother?" her daughter asks.

"Oh, I feel so stupid." Above her head on the wall is a fancy framed photograph with Solomon and his dog, Cathy. There's also a small bulletin board with dozens of photos of pets, pets and their owners, litters of dogs, and paintings or drawings of pets, and a framed poem entitled "The Precious Gifts He Gives, A Tribute to Dr. Gene Solomon."

Solomon calls for a technician to retrieve the dog so that a few tests can be conducted, and then addresses the woman and her daughter about the many years of intestinal disease that their dog has suffered and how a consistent proper diet would help stabilize the dog's health—and increase its longevity. They spend a good deal of time discussing animals and nutrition, trading questions, answers, and ideas until the woman interrupts by asking, "What about grapes?"

"Well," says Solomon, continuing to be sincere and matter-of-fact simultaneously, without indicating signs of annoyance, "a springer spaniel's ideal diet will probably not include grapes . . ."

Now the woman addresses her daughter: "I really have to get Joel to stop feeding her French food on Saturday afternoon."

Solomon interjects: "I actually have less of a problem with croissants than I do fried chicken."

The woman looks up, hopefully. "So croissants are good for dogs then?"

"I wouldn't go that far," Solomon says.

By recording conversation, the creative nonfiction writer captures reality. This is how people communicate in everyday life. The interference of a reporter attempting to sound authentic while maintaining objectivity is eliminated. As in fiction writing, dialogue enhances action and characterization, while eliciting reader reaction through humor (as in the above example) or tragedy.

Here is a conversation between two distressed people at a breaking point in their lives, from my book, *Stuck in Time*.

It begins in social worker Debbie Rubin's office as she meets with Tom and Elizabeth Scanlon, whose daughter, Meggan, is mentally ill. Because of insurance limitations, Meggan cannot stay at Western Psych, a hospital that has been helpful to Meggan in the past, and there are few options remaining, none of which seems workable. Technically, Meggan can return home, but Tom and Elizabeth have decided that this is unacceptable. They are ready to relinquish custody, if CYS (Children's and Youth Services) and Orphan's Court will allow such an action. Even if relinquishment is permitted, who will guarantee that Meggan is placed in a desirable facility? For that matter, does a desirable facility exist for Meggan Scanlon? And where will Meggan live until she can be placed? Time is running out for Tom and Elizabeth. The only interim solution is a transfer to Mayview State Hospital, which would be inappropriate.

"You look good in black," Tom Scanlon tells Debbie Rubin, as he settles into his seat, opposite her desk. Rubin smiles and swivels back and forth in her chair. In addition to her black suit, she is wearing new red shoes. I know they are new because I have never seen them before, and over the past year I have been in a position to notice a great number of Debbie Rubin's shoes. From my vantage point across the room, behind Debbie and opposite Tom and Elizabeth, I have noted that Debbie hides her feet under her desk and slips off her shoes whenever her therapy sessions become difficult. When she turns toward the Scanlons, her face will remain impassive despite the intensity of the experience, the sadness, or the confrontation that she will sometimes precipitate, but her toes are preoccupied—twirling, dangling, tangoing with her shoes.

Rubin is 40 years old. She has an eight-year-old son whose photograph sits in a gold and silver frame on her desk; her husband is a cardiologist at a large community hospital two miles from campus. Rubin was born and educated in Pittsburgh, but a dozen years ago moved with her husband to Boston, where she first worked as a psychiatric social worker. Following her husband back to Pittsburgh, she was offered a position on 3 West, the adolescent unit. Her father had been a social worker at

Western Psych; he retired in 1976 as director of the Social Work Department.

Elizabeth initiates the discussion by pointing out that Meggan continues to insist she is going home after her discharge from Western Psych. If they cannot get her into a special school or group or foster home through CYS in Pittsburgh, however, Elizabeth is contemplating a move to North Carolina, where her sister lives and where services for emotionally disturbed children are more readily available.

Suddenly, Elizabeth points her finger and speaks to Debbie Rubin accusingly: "If you make me take Meggan back home this time, I swear to God . . . ." She pauses and takes a deep breath. "I won't take her back home—no."

Elizabeth takes a deep breath and begins again, taking a different tack. She says that it is becoming increasingly important to her that Meggan learn to achieve something—anything—at school, any school. "I am not looking for too much. I don't need her to become president of the United States or a brain surgeon. But she used to have such energy!

"Meggan is a terrific student. If you were a teacher, you would kill for a student like my daughter. She's creative, she's exciting—she's weird. She's always been appreciated more by adults than by the kids her own age, and she usually hooked herself into her favorite teacher. The kids thought she was strange. Well, for God's sake, I knew more than anyone how strange and weird she was. But I have always fought for her right to be different." Now tears are rolling down Elizabeth's cheeks. "Meggan is telling people in the unit that she is a vampire. This is her way of acknowledging that she will be forever different."

Debbie Rubin passes a box of Kleenex. Elizabeth nods appreciatively and dabs her eyes.

"And when is the worst possible time in life to feel different?" Rubin asks.

"When you are a teenager."

"What do you think Meggan is going to say when she

learns that she is really not coming home—that your willingness to relinquish your parental rights is for real?"

"I know that Meggan knows that I love her. And that is a heck of a big step from one generation to another because when I was her age, my mother never made me feel that way. But," Elizabeth adds, "your question is only theoretical. I don't have any confidence that she is not going to come home—despite what you say." Once again, Elizabeth looks accusingly at Debbie Rubin.

"I don't know what to say to you about sending Meggan to Mayview or anywhere else," says Rubin. "I don't have the answers right now."

Elizabeth began describing the joyous state of their lives with Meggan out of the house. "We have a wonderful family when the three of us—me and Tom and Doug—are together. Doug thinks I am a great mother."

"Doug and I have never been closer," says Tom.

"He's our pride and joy. He gets into trouble from time to time, but he tells us the truth. Meg insults us."

"What does it take to convince people to get her off the streets?" Tom asks. "Does she need to be gang-raped? Should we let her kill someone with a car?"

"If we had enough money our problems would be solved," said Elizabeth. "But there's nothing left; no college money, no savings. It all went to Meggan's therapists and her private schools." The Scanlons are $42,000 in debt, "completely at risk every day of our lives."

Tom sighs, squirms, and turns to face the wall. "I have to abandon my daughter in order to receive public services? I guess I haven't paid my taxes all these years."

"I can't understand why you refuse to refer her to Mayview," Elizabeth says to Debbie Rubin.

"It is not clear to me that Meggan is not going to Mayview," Rubin replies calmly.

"What I have always hoped is that someone would take her away from us and take care of her," says Elizabeth. "But after North Country, I wished she was dead." She pauses to snatch another Kleenex and wipe her eyes.

"In lieu of that—I mean instead of killing her, which is what I really want to do—I have decided to leave. To leave Tom, to leave Meggan, to leave Doug—everybody. It's not pretty, it's not right, but that's all there is. I have begged for help. I have demanded help. But I can't do it anymore. I can't go on. I'm leaving home."

"I have been watching you out of the corner of my eye," Debbie says to Tom. "What are you thinking?"

"I am sitting here listening to my death sentence," he replies.

"Yours or Meggan's?"

"If Meggan comes home, Elizabeth will leave me. I feel like someone is passing a life sentence over me for a crime I did not commit."

Tom remembers the last time Elizabeth left him—an incident precipitated by the same question with which they are attempting to deal today: What to do with Meggan? It had occurred the summer following her expulsion from North Country. Because of continued warfare between the two children, Doug and Meggan could not be at home alone at the same time, and the Scanlons had exhausted their pool of babysitters willing to go head-to-head with Meggan. Because Doug was younger, it was easier to find child care for him outside the home, although at thirteen, he had had enough.

"One afternoon, Douglas and I were having a rather loud discussion about the problem," said Elizabeth. "I was upset and he was upset and we weren't coming to any good conclusions. Meggan suddenly started telling me how I should have handled the situation."

Elizabeth had always known deep in her heart that sooner or later she would reach a point of no return—a moment when her daughter's unyielding assaults upon her would force her either to lose her mind entirely or to flee.

Meggan had always been able to hurt her by instinctively saying the things to which Elizabeth was most sensitive. "I've talked to other mothers with kids like Meggan. They all relate the same kind of thing. Sometimes you know damn well you did wrong, but it's extraordinarily painful to listen to." Ordinarily Elizabeth would have fought back, or locked herself in her room. But Meggan had picked the absolute worst moment to launch an attack. "I left the house and moved in with a girlfriend."

Although Tom understood that Elizabeth had reached a breaking point—and needed respite from Meggan—the days he remained alone as a single parent had been devastating. "There were days when I went to work and could barely function. The night that Elizabeth left I just sat and cried the whole night. Meggan made fun of me. She said, 'You're acting like a jerk. She'll be back. What are you worried about?' Doug was as upset as I was. He went into his room and cried. I sat on the bed and cried with him. Meg went out and chose not to come home until midnight without telling me where she was going. I could have just killed her." Tom snaps a Kleenex from the box and dabs the tears from his eyes. He buries his face in his hands.

"I simply have to get away because I get afraid that I'm just going to die, that this situation with Meggan is going to kill me, that she is killing my soul," says Elizabeth. "It sounds really awful. I feel helpless and out of control. I can barely talk when Meggan is home, because I don't have anything to offer her anymore. I visualize myself as one of the shadows on the street after the bombing of Nagasaki and Hiroshima. I saw the pictures of those people who were just mere shadows on the pavement. That's how empty I felt when I had left Tom. I felt like there was nothing there. I had no presence. I was a shadow on the pavement. I had to get out."

"My best friend is divorced. She's been on her own for years. She goes home every night to a quiet apartment and plays whatever she wants on the radio—something wonderful. You go over there and it's quiet. Oh my God! I can remember going to see her at lunch and crying and saying, 'I want your life. I just want your whole life. I'll give up everything else. Let me have it.' It's becoming harder and harder to function, to get through the day. I have to get . . . ." She searches for the words, but Rubin finds them:

"You have to get away from Meggan—your daughter."

"That's right."

"And you are willing to sacrifice your relationship with Tom?"

"I will never sacrifice my relationship with Tom. But don't you see? My feeling for Tom is deep inside of me, and it will never go away. Practically, I can live without him."

"But can Tom live without being with you?"

"No, he can't."

"So what is going to happen to Tom if you leave?"

"What is going to happen to me," asks Elizabeth, "if I stay?"

Debbie Rubin's shoes have been on and off four times in the past ten minutes. Her voice becomes high-pitched during such tense moments, and she has the tendency to press her chin on her fist and mumble, forcing Tom to lean forward. "I can't hear you," he says.

"The sad part about all of this," says Rubin, repeating herself, "is that your guilt over giving up Meggan is not going to go away even if you are successful in placing her somewhere. You will both always feel like beasts."

"She makes me feel like a hostage," says Elizabeth. "Any moment, she is going to take her hot poker out and burn me again. I can't explain it to people. She makes me feel like a battered wife. I can't deal with her. I can't deal with a child who relishes my hurt. The more that I hurt, the happier she is. There ought to be shelters for battered mothers to protect them from their children. I cannot continually be terrorized by a child. The cost is too high."

"So listen to me," says Debbie Rubin. "I think that the one person who has gotten you through all of this is Tom."

"That's absolutely true," says Elizabeth.

"But you want to leave him?"

"Tom can't protect me from her. He wants to, but he can't." Elizabeth raises her voice. "I won't look for a new husband, and he won't be looking for a new wife. I will be with him in heart and spirit for the rest of my life."

She is sobbing hysterically. She begins to choke. The four of us sit in silence while she calms herself. "Life wasn't really supposed to be this hard. It really wasn't," she finally says.

"We will work together and do all we can to accomplish your objective. We will make phone calls to anyone who will listen. We will fight the fight together," Rubin tells them.

"What kind of time frame are we talking until you send her home?" Tom asks abruptly.

Rubin remains calm, but she is clearly perplexed. "I keep trying to tell you that I don't know that we are going to send her home. We're talking the worst-case scenario—home. We know that we can keep her for another month—we have our ways to do that, to sway the insurance company. And there's a chance to get her into Mayview for anywhere from three to nine months. And then maybe group homes."

Tom's face is red and wet. His voice is choked and weak. "For Godsake, Debbie, get her in there—to Mayview. Get her anywhere. Just for a while. Please."

"Maybe we should sell the house and move into an apartment, take all the money that's left and send her to school for one more year," says Elizabeth.

"I'll do that, happily," says Tom. "I'll do anything," he adds.

Now Tom is sobbing. Elizabeth is crying quietly. Debbie Rubin watches them both, playing with her shoes and pressing her fist into her face.

Tom says,"I have never been happier in my life than I have been with Elizabeth."

"Then you have to fight for what you want, Tom," Debbie Rubin says.

"I'm trying," says Tom. "I am fighting with all my power."

"There's a limit to my strength," says Elizabeth. "I must have peace."

"How peaceful will it be without Tom?"

"The only other solution that I can think of is suicide," says Elizabeth.*

3.3   "Inner" Point of View

Note that these conversations not only contain description—what is happening in the room and what the characters look like as they talk—but also an inner point of view. In other words, readers see the world through the eyes of the characters whose lives are being dramatized.

The veterinarian scene vividly portrays Dr. Solomon, who is clearly going through the motions of supplying the best service to a client who is not particularly considerate of a pet she truly loves. But the creative nonfiction writer can also take the opportunity to capture a character's feelings directly:

As we leave the examination room and walk down the hall toward his office, Solomon's face reddens and he shakes his head with disgust. "How many times has she been here?" he says, flipping the pages of the chart. "Twenty times? Thirty times? And what's the first question I asked her on her first visit?" he flips back to the beginning of the chart. "Diet. 'What do you feed your dog?' We go through this every time at anywhere from $75 to $250 a visit. And she will not listen. I would pay her the $75 or $250 if she would only listen—just once."

*From Lee Gutkind, *Stuck in Time*, © 1993. Reprinted by permission of Henry Holt and Company, Inc.

In the Scanlon scene, you feel and see the confusion and panic as you view the awful frustration of their lives through their own eyes. You also hear Elizabeth's agonized threat of suicide. But to elongate tension and point of view, there can be a second or third scenic "twist."

> With the exception of playing with her shoes, Debbie Rubin has skillfully led the session without exhibiting a great deal of emotion. She has been warm, attentive, and responsive. Even now, Rubin does not change her expression. She maintains eye contact with the distraught mother. Rubin knows that suicide is not a new idea for Elizabeth, for she has previously admitted to Debbie that she considers death a viable option to living with Meggan. But this time, she has added another frightening wrinkle to her destructive scenario.
>
> "You would leave Tom and Doug with that legacy of suicide?" Rubin asks her.
>
> "No," says Elizabeth calmly. "My new idea is that we will all three make the choice of going together."

Remember: The creative nonfiction writer may not employ "literary license"—the writer may not alter truth to enhance the story or the dramatic narrative. In other words, writers cannot create conversations that did not happen—or even dramatically embellish upon those that did happen. But in creative nonfiction, the writer is encouraged to capture the drama and force of real life, in the most literary way possible.

The creative nonfiction writer is encouraged to utilize all the literary techniques available to the fiction writer in order to render his or her true story as dramatic, appealing, and compelling as possible.

Scenes: The Building Blocks of Creative Nonfiction

4.1   The Yellow Test

Scenes (vignettes, episodes, slices of reality, and so forth) are the building blocks of creative nonfiction—the primary factor that separates and defines literary and/or creative nonfiction from traditional journalism and ordinary lifeless prose.

The uninspired writer will *tell* the reader about a subject, place, or personality, but the creative nonfiction writer will *show* that subject, place, or personality in action. Before we discuss the actual content or construction of a scene, let me suggest that you perform what I like to call the yellow test.

Take a yellow highlighting marker and leaf through some of your favorite magazines—*Vanity Fair, Esquire, The New Yorker* or the journal I edit, *Creative Nonfiction.* Or return to favorite chapters in those previously mentioned books—*Jaws, The Bridges of Madison County, House, This Boy's Life, The Red Badge of Courage.*

Highlight the scenes, just the scenes, long and short. Then go back to the beginning and review your handiwork. Chances are that anywhere from 75 percent to 95 percent of each essay, short story, or novel selected will be yellow. Plays are obviously constructed with scenes, as are films. Most poems are very scenic.

There's nothing fancy about a scene, by the way. A scene is a story. The examples in this book are all scenes—in Gene Solomon's examination room, on the Skyline Drive on the motorcycle, in the psychiatrist's sanctuary with the Scanlons—all scenes. Do a yellow test with the Readings in the back of this book: scenes. As the Pulitzer Prize-winning author David McCullough once said: "Writing a book is not as complicated as it seems; it's just a series of stories."

4.2   Integrating Scenes

As a reader, you may not have noticed the proliferation of scenes until now. Good writers understand that craft—the techniques they employ—must remain ever so subtle, so that the writing itself never gets in the way of the story they are attempting to tell. Readers should not be aware of the fact that they are reading scenes. The idea behind writing in scenes is to make the prose flow so smoothly that readers are entranced, living the experience about which they are reading.

Here's an example of a series of scenes or stories knitted subtly together, but in a logical and chronological pattern. Try my "yellowing" technique, then count the actual scenes embedded in this one story.

> Orthopedic surgery is not always the answer when a horse loses its ability to race at full speed or its will to gallop aggressively and win; in fact, surgeons at New Bolton have developed a number of highly sophisticated diagnostic tools in order to understand the often subtle and complicated reasons why horses experience difficulty on the race track.
>
> The horse Eric Parente has been asked to evaluate is a quitter. This horse goes like hell for five-sixths of the race and then, just about the time the owners are counting their money and computing their profits, he slows down. Parente, a 32-year-old veterinarian, a graduate of Cornell School of Veterinary Medicine whose specialty is sports medicine, is muscular and well-built, with thick brown hair lightly speckled with gray, a square jaw, and a row of perfect teeth.

His office is a mess. There are sweat clothes and running shoes stashed under his desk. He's wearing basketball shoes, white socks, khakis, and a light blue shirt with a New Bolton emblem on it. The shirt is significantly wrinkled after a long semi-sleepless night.

Among other interests, Parente has been focusing his attention upon the many problems having to do with lameness in the hock, which is a common ailment for horses. Hocks are like human ankles. Steroids are usually used to treat these problems, Parente says. "The cheaper horses get more steroids because they're not going to win many races, so the owners race them and forget them, whereas for a more expensive horse an owner will invest the money to permanently heal the lameness and eradicate the pain."

As we walk from his office to the Jeffords Treadmill Facility, Parente discusses the horse we are going to see, a chocolate brown three-year-old with a brown mane and one white foot who seems to slow down at the home stretch, the point at which he should be barreling at top speed. Preliminary examination has ruled out obvious problems, such as lameness.

First, Parente must grind off the traction-inducing toe grabs on the horse's shoes, which would tear into the rubber of the treadmill. For this he uses a large carpenter's sander with extra coarse sandpaper. He shows the grinder to the horse and triggers it so that the horse can become familiar with its sound—and also learn to trust him. He places his hand on the horse, and he holds on when the horse tries to jerk away. In a persistently gentle manner, Parente holds on tightly until the horse is comfortable with his touch.

I've observed him practice a similar philosophy with the horse's mouth during a dental examination. "Hold on, allow them to make their objections. But be relaxed and firm at the same time," he says. Horses, Parente explained, have incisors in the front and molars in the back of their mouths—and an interdental space in the middle. "So if your psychology fails, and they decide to bite down with your hands in their mouth, your fingers will be safe if you keep them in the interdental space. As an added safeguard, a veterinarian can reposition a horse's tongue to the side so that it lies between molars. Then, if they do get testy and chomp down it will be on their own tongues, and they will be in much more pain than you. In that way, you can examine one side of the mouth in relative safety. Then flip the tongue back to the other side of the mouth and complete your examination."

Now Parente slowly creeps under the horse, lifts its front leg at the hock, and begins to grind. The noise is disturbing to the horse, as are the fiery metal sparks, which he carefully directs away from any contact with the horse. Leg coverings have been wrapped around the horse below the knee, but despite the three students holding it and attempting to keep it relatively still, the horse rears up and kicks, a hoof whizzing past Parente's shoulder as he jumps away.

They try again. This time they employ a tool made of an ax handle with a loop of clothesline at the end. The loop is fitted around the horse's nose, and the ax handle is twisted until the horse is brought under control. It's called a twitch, as in "Do you want me to 'twitch' him, Dr. Parente?"

After the grinding, the horse is allowed to become accustomed to the treadmill by walking around it, sniffing and nudging it with his nose. Then he is led up the ramp and onto the matted rubber floor; eventually he is tethered up against a breastplate. The speed of the running surface is controlled from a console.

The treadmill simulates racing conditions. At a top speed of 37 miles per hour its running surface is elevated to an uphill slope of six degrees, which forces animals to work harder. For diagnostic procedures, the animal is worked up to 200 to 240 heart beats per minute, the heart rate at racing speed. In the process, sports medicine clinicians compile an impressive broadside of tests, including cardiovascular evaluation utilizing a radio telemetric heart monitor. An endoscope, inserted into the horse's throat through a nostril, reveals the larynx, viewed on a large TV screen to detect irregularities that may shed light on the "noisy breathing" of a racer, a sign that a horse's airway is somehow being restricted.

Other crucial measurements compiled while the horse is running include oxygen consumption, CO_2 and lactic acid production, respiratory and upper airway flow, blood and venous pressures, blood gases, glucose metabolism, and oxygenation. These measurements are fed into three computers that are located in the diagnostic laboratory adjacent to the treadmill. In addition to two stalls, the centerpiece of the building is a twelve-windowed steeple braced by two magnificent arches that rise dramatically to the ceiling. "It's kind of like the Sistine Chapel," Parente says.

The treadmill, made by Walmanik International Corporation in Freedom, PA, is fully enclosed by bulletproof polycarbonate in case a horse loses a shoe while galloping. Perhaps one thousand standardbred and thoroughbred horses have been evaluated on this treadmill since the diagnostic center was opened in 1992. "I guess you could find out what's wrong with this horse sooner or later by trial and error, but the investment in time and energy might be prohibitive," Parente says.

Now the treadmill is activated, allowing the horse to walk, at first slowly and then more briskly. Gradually, the horse is led into a slow and steady trot, lasting just a few minutes. The pace is reduced, then once again increased. This time the horse is worked from a walk to a trot to a canter. It is amusing to observe the horse orient himself to the treadmill. The floor suddenly starts to move beneath him, but he is amazed to discover that the walls are staying right where they are.

The horse steps gingerly on the moving tread, as if attempting to clutch the ground with nonexistent toes. Attendants have been stationed on both sides of the horse to steady and control him with guide ropes. Once in a while, the horse bristles. His pace breaks. A couple of taps on the rear with a crop by one of the attendants reminds him to resume his unhurried canter.

The space beneath the treadmill is hollow, and the hooves striking the tread make deep, full-timbered drumbeats. As the horse's speed increases, hooves pounding, the intensity infects everybody gathered in the complex, students, observers, and clinicians alike. But before the horse reaches his galloping peak of power, the pace is eased again. The horse is bathed and rested. An hour later, the official test begins.

The horse ran two miles in the warm-up phase, but the test will be about two and a half miles long—and much more intense. While waiting, Parente shows me videotapes of a racing horse's normal breathing rhythm recorded by the endoscope. "Before having the capacity to videotape the action in the epiglottis, veterinarians would have to interview jockeys about the 'noisy breathing' a horse was making. Or the vet had to sit on a rail and listen as the horse galloped by."

Since joining the treadmill diagnostic team and identifying and repairing breathing problems, which has become a special interest, Parente has had one horse achieve a lifetime speed mark. "I look at the newspaper from time to time to see who's racing, and I often recognize the names of the winners as horses I worked on. That's a great payback."

Another payback is closer to his heart: As a young boy, Parente's father spent a great deal of time at the racetrack with a favorite great aunt. Inspired by his father's stories,

Parente chose veterinary medicine as a career and equine surgery as a specialty, even though he has hardly ever ridden a horse. Even now, six years out of veterinary school, he suspects he hasn't been in the saddle ten times in his entire life. His father is uncomfortable leading a horse on a leash. But Parente, his father, brother or mother are not the least bit uncomfortable buying and racing thoroughbred horses.

The family started with a $5,000 cheap claimer and is now involved in the upper echelon of horse racing known as "stakes racing" as owners of a two-year-old thoroughbred whose grandfather is the famed triple-crown winner, Seattle Slew. Their thoroughbred's father is named Houston, and Parente's father's nickname for his favorite great aunt was Ziz. Thus, their horse acquired his name, Tex Ziz Slew. Parente, who is engaged to an equine veterinarian he met at Cornell, is happy with his work and his life. "The horses are athletes. And the challenge is both physical and intellectual. You try to finesse rather than overpower the animal. To me, that's what racing and training is all about."

Soon the quitter is brought back onto the treadmill. The breastplate in front of the horse is removed, because the team has found that when horses begin to flat-out gallop, they sometimes get so carried away that they want to try to jump over it. Now everyone gathers around, positioning themselves in front of a monitor. Then an attendant steps forward, placing the twitch on the horse, as Parente inserts the endoscope tube into the horse's nostril for the videotape of the throat. Now the twitch is removed. The treadmill elevation is increased three degrees. The horse walks, trots, canters—and then explodes into a sustained gallop.

Against the black tread of the floor, the brown hooves are lost in the blur of his gallop; all we can see after a while is the flash of a single white hoof. His mane is bouncing against his neck. The thundering sound is deafening. The horse begins to snort. He is being slapped on the butt with a crop from both sides now. His body is strained. His muscles are flexing. His eyes are glazed over with excitement. A technician is yelling out numbers as she glances back and forth at the heart monitor. A veterinarian visiting from Ohio State University is bellowing "Hup! Hup!" Someone else begins to yell "Yahoo!" The scene is hypnotic. Everyone is either screaming or stomping their feet.

Suddenly, at the two-mile mark, something happens. A subtle measure of intensity in the horse seems to dissipate. Did he lose momentum? Did that stallion, that gallant racer, in fact quit? He is slapped several more times with the crops, but clearly something significant has occurred. The treadmill slows down, gradually. The test is over. The veterinarian from Ohio State applauds.

Immediately Eric Parente goes to the videotape, rewinds it, and plays it back. "Here's the problem." The horse is displacing his palate, which folds up over the epiglottis and partially restricts breathing. "Listen to the sound," Parente says, turning up the volume. "Hear it? *Huh, huh, huh.* His airway closes down on him from time to time, and he's struggling, can't expire fully, and since he can't expire fully, he also can't get a fresh full swallow of air. So when he breathes in, half of the air he's trying to breathe has already been used. It's all here on the tape," Parente concludes.

Is "noisy breathing" the same as "roaring"?

"A roarer," he explains, "can't open his arytenoid all the way because of fatigue. When a horse is going full-tilt both arytenoids should remain completely open. A horse will roar when one collapses and shuts down." The arytenoid flaps every time the horse breathes in, the way the swinging door to a cowboy saloon flaps when anyone enters the room. A couple of different surgical procedures are used to help silence the roaring horse. One is a laryngoplasty, which involves tying back the arytenoid so that the paralyzed vocal chord is removed from the airway. Sports medicine surgeons at New Bolton will perform about 100 of these procedures a year.

Officially, the quitter's diagnosis is dorsal displacement of the soft palate. It's a functional problem in the throat as compared to a structural problem, which means that it may be more difficult to repair. Parente will suggest a minor procedure that has been borrowed by veterinarians from pediatric surgeons. For children with aphonia, who cannot trigger enough vibration in their vocal chords to make a noise, a liquid Teflon-like material is injected under the epiglottis. Scar tissue is formed, stiffening the bottom of the epiglottis.

The tool utilized for the procedure resembles a caulking gun with a long needle. Pediatric surgeons inject the Teflon in this way through the mouths of children who are under anesthesia. "We do it with an incision underneath the larynx. You couldn't ever reach the epiglottis through the horse's mouth. We've had relatively good success with this procedure for horses who displace," Parente concludes. "This may not be the horse's only problem, but it is a partial answer to the owner's nagging question: 'Why does this horse quit?'"

How many of those crucial building blocks called "scenes" come together to be integrated into one overall story? Again, much depends on how you define or isolate the scene, but here's a pretty safe break-down, beginning with the statement of the problem—the horse is a quitter. From Parente's office (1) to grinding the quitter's shoes and "twitching" (2); checking out the treadmill (3); activating treadmill—first run (4); second run (5); wild gallop and then the horse suddenly quits (6); Parente's diagnosis: Why this horse quits.

Perform the yellow test on the essays in the Readings section. Count the scenes—you'll be surprised at how many you discover. There are more than a dozen in Donald Morrill's "I Give Up Smiling," in a voyage that takes the reader worldwide, while Margaret Gibson is equally scenic although her story takes place mostly in rural Virginia. In fact, while you are reading and counting, block out the dialogue and description in order to see how scenes are constructed and how, once those scenes are intact, they are integrated into a larger story.

4.3   Leads Thrust the Reader into the Essay

We live in a very cinematic culture. We don't go to a movie theatre anymore—it's now called a cineplex—and there are often a dozen feature films from which to choose. In the livingroom at home, we channel surf, and in our office, we browse the Internet. A viewer's (and a reader's) eye is attuned to movement, action, a three-dimensional experience. In addition, the competition for the busy reader's attention is heated. This is one of the reasons that writers attempt to be as scenic as possible, whenever possible, to catch the attention of the reader and to convince the reader that you (the writer) have something to say.

Leafing through a magazine, a reader will see the title of an article or essay, and it might interest him or her to begin browsing or scanning the first few words. The reader will read a paragraph—perhaps two—during which time a decision will be formulating in his or her mind. The reader will ask, What is this essay or article about? Am I interested in this subject? Am I willing to devote 30 minutes (or three hours) of my precious time to this writer's work? At some point, fairly quickly, a reader commits or rejects your work, continuing to read or moving on to something else.

It is impossible to underestimate the importance of the first few paragraphs in an essay. They must be cinematically compelling and substantively communicative, getting readers involved in the action of the scenic narrative while informing them about what they will be learning. The idea is to grab readers and thrust them into the heat of the action, before any other essay or article attracts their attention, as is done in the first paragraph of "The Garden in Winter" from Readings:

This was supposed to be the weekend I put my garden to
bed for winter—time to clip the lilac suckers, mulch some
perennials and tuck in a few last bulbs—but instead I'm on a

train to Philadelphia to say goodbye to a friend who is dying. I had planned for my hands to be happily immersed in dirt, but then I got the call asking, "Will you come hold my hand?" She never asked me to hold her hand before. I'm thinking about her, and my garden, and suddenly I'm reconfirming my resolve to specialize in perennials, plants that only pretend to die. They surprise you each spring with a resurrection you never really expect, but then there it is.

The triumph in this lead is that it is dramatic and suspenseful (Who is this friend and why is she dying? Will the narrator make it to Philadelphia on time?). We know simultaneously that the friend and the garden are metaphoric: The theme is not subtle; it strikes home. This lead also contains dialogue and a bit of description. All in all, this is a small package—with a big impact. The first chapter of *Stuck in Time: The Tragedy of Childhood Mental Illness* accomplishes the same objective for a book-length work.

When I drove up to the house, Daniel was walking toward me. I got out of the car and waited for him to approach. Even though he waved and flashed a quick smile, he seemed grim and befuddled. "What's wrong, Dan?"

He shrugged and shook his head as we walked up the steps toward the porch. "Nothing's wrong," he said. But his eyes were darting erratically from side to side.

Daniel had been working periodically that summer at a rental property I owned, cleaning out the basement, a filthy job that he savored. Nothing made Daniel happier than getting dirty, especially with a bunch of junk. A pack rat, Daniel had always rummaged through trash, rescuing an array of mechanical objects—manual typewriters, speedometers, radios, lamps, rusty tools, old motors. Keys of any size, shape, or condition were his special passion, and locks, whether or not they corresponded to the keys. Sometimes he managed to clean or fix a derelict item of junk and sell it at a Sunday flea market, but usually Daniel was more interested in contemplating these items in the questionable safety of his room.

Daniel is short and broad, part muscle from his recent forays into weight lifting and part paunch from overeating. It was not unusual for him to devour a large pizza with sausage, mushroom, and pepperoni—our traditional Saturday afternoon snack—followed by a few hot sausage hoagies for dinner. Over the past few years, he had changed a good deal physically; when he was twelve, he weighed 90 pounds, a frail and exceedingly delicate feather of a boy; now, still very short, he could more aptly be described as a fireplug.

We stopped at the top of the steps, and I put my hands on his shoulders. Ruffling his curly hair with my hand, I joked about how dirty he was and made a crack about his ears, which are unusually small. I could almost always get him to laugh by invoking his ears or by pointing out that he was most handsome on Halloween when he wore a mask. But this time he did not laugh or protest; he was so somber that I pulled him down on the stoop and looked him straight in the eye. "C'mon Dan, something's wrong; what's going on?"

Although I could see it coming, I was surprised at the power of his emotions. A mask of fear suddenly exploded onto his face, and he began to whine like a small, frightened child. "Oh, I'm so scared. He's going to kill me."

His eyes darted crazily, and he tried to stand up and run, but I held onto him. "I won't let anyone hurt you."

Tears were streaming down his face, which were buried in my chest. "A man molested me." He reached down and began squeezing his buttocks. "Oh, it hurts," he wailed. "It hurts so bad back there."

Another way of enticing a reader is to start with a scene designed for dramatic impact, as in Margaret Gibson's mention of Boston Blackie in "Thou Shalt Not Kill" in the Readings section. Blackie on TV establishes a mood, but the first real scene, at least as it relates to the story being told, is when Edwin kills a chicken.

Both methods can and do work. The objective is to start a story and introduce the main characters and the conflict in which they are involved or the problem that confronts them—in an action-oriented manner. In this manner, a good lead manipulates and compels the reader to read further.

4.4   Reading with a Double Perspective

This might be the time to point out the difference between reading as a reader and reading as a writer.

As writers, we must learn to read the products we produce through the eyes of the people we are trying to reach. This is how editors choose the essays, articles, or books they decide to publish. It is not only what they, personally, like to read that counts, although that is an important factor. What will appeal to their readers also matters.

If you were a buyer for a department store, a manufacturer's representative might come to see you with a sample case full of shoes. You might be impressed with the style and quality of the products the salesperson presents, but before you buy you must be convinced that your customers will be equally impressed, so much so that they will buy enough of the shoes to allow for a healthy profit for your company. Analogously, you must learn to analyze your essay through a reader's eye.

However, what we are doing in this book, more than anything else, is learning to examine our work with a *writer's* eye to understand the elements or the architecture of creative nonfiction. Engineers, for instance, will examine a bridge in two distinctively different ways: First, they will consider how it looks from the surface, to the people who will walk or drive across the bridge. Then, their eyes will dig deeper, noting and evaluating the structural pattern and integrity of the edifice.

Similarly, the writer should visualize the structural elements of essays, chapters, books, and so forth, in order to achieve intellectual harmony with the work, specifically, and the reader, generally. The architecture of the essay—the structural integrity—begins with the repeated use of scenes.

4.5   The Elements of a Scene

Words and concepts to remember: Scenes are the building blocks of creative nonfiction. Scenes specifically and creative nonfiction generally are action-oriented, cinematic, three dimensional. They may contain all the devices through which the best fiction is constructed, including dialogue, description, point of view, and specificity and intimacy of detail.

Scenes move the narrative forward and compel the reader to stay involved.

Scenes are dramatic; they often pose a conflict that promises resolution, which is another reason a reader will remain involved. The conflict is established immediately in the Solomon scene when he asks,

"Tell me what you feed her." The woman gulps and lowers her head.

Now the reader will want to know why the woman is embarrassed. This is the same conflict Jeanne Marie Laskas establishes when she says,

I'm thinking about her, and my garden, and suddenly I'm reconfirming my resolve to specialize in perennials, plants that only pretend to die.

It is the same conflict in "The Quitter" who

. . . goes like hell for five-sixths of the race and then, just about the time the owners are counting their money and computing their profits, he slows down.

Scenes are pictures; they are cinematic representations of reality, which elicit curiosity and excitement, enticing the reader onward.

In this age of TV and video culture, a writer must evoke a three-dimensional portrait of the subject about which he or she is writing.

Scenes contain specificity and intimacy of detail. This is something I have not yet discussed, but it is a crucial yet subtle element in high quality literature.

4.6   Intimate Detail

To make scenes seem authentic and special, writers attempt to include memorable small or unusual details that readers would not necessarily know or even imagine. A very famous intimate detail appears in a classic creative nonfiction profile of Frank Sinatra written by Gay Talese in 1962 and published in *Esquire* magazine. In this profile, Talese leads us on a whirlwind cross-country tour, revealing Sinatra and his entourage interacting with one another and with the rest of the world, and demonstrating how the Sinatra world and the world inhabited by everyone else will often collide.

These scenes are action oriented; they contain dialogue and evocative description with great specificity and intimacy of detail, such as the gray-haired lady spotted in the shadows of the Sinatra entourage—the guardian of Sinatra's collection of toupees. This tiny detail—Sinatra's wig lady—loomed so large in my mind when I first read the essay that even now, 35 years later, anytime I see Sinatra on TV or spot his photo in a magazine, I find myself unconsciously searching the background for the gray-haired lady with the hatbox.

Look for intimate details in excerpts of essays and books published in this section and in the Readings. Here is a sample from Margaret Gibson. This is good descriptive writing, but we also learn special details we would not necessarily know or easily imagine:

> I saw Edwin in front of the open shed, in baggy overalls, no
> shirt on. He was Marie's husband. A hen fluttered and
> squawked in one of his hands. He had her by the ankle part
> of her legs, and her yellow feet stuck out the back of a hand
> as big as a baseball mitt. Sun flashed off the head of the

hatchet that hung in the ring of his overalls. I stopped still and watched him intently. What was he doing? He was whistling.

4.7   The Art and Craft of Creative Nonfiction

The writing process is not a scientific endeavor, despite my emphasis on the anatomy or architecture of the essay. The writing process contains two integral parts, beginning with an essential spontaneity, which is the cornerstone of the creative experience.

Poets, composers, and sculptors do not create by thinking about the basic structures and patterns in their craft, such as rhyme, meter, shape, and so forth. This is inherent, ingrained knowledge—something they feel or know instinctively and have studied and contemplated over the years.

Superstar athletes—baseball players, basketball players, tennis stars—study forehands, foul shots, fielding techniques. But during a game or match, their bodies perform spontaneously. After a game, they will isolate their mistakes by studying a videotape or using other evaluation tools. So will sculptors or composers who refine spontaneous creative efforts. But during the process of playing (writing, creating, and so forth), an instinctive fluidity is necessarily let loose.

Similarly, in the creative nonfiction writing process, the anatomy or architecture of the essay eventually should be ingrained so that the writer instinctively conceptualizes scenes, stories, dialogue, and so forth and applies them during the writing effort. After the spontaneously creative effort, during the many necessary revisions, structure and craft come into play more directly.

Framing

5.1 The Convoluted Story

Pulp Fiction, Quentin Tarantino's brilliant, violent Academy Award-winning (Best Screenplay) film, actually begins in a diner with a conversation between two psychopathic lovers who, in the course of eating breakfast, decide to stage a holdup, stealing money from the cash register and from all the customers.

But before the viewer knows whether the crime ever takes place, Tarantino flashes back 24 hours to introduce a number of key characters involved tangentially in a smarmy web of drug-induced corruption and murder.

In a series of tautly paced and powerful scenes, Tarantino plunges the film's stars, Bruce Willis, John Travolta, Samuel Jackson, Harvey Keitel, Uma Thurman, Roseanna Arquette, and Eric Stoltz, into situations that lead to dangerous conflict in each of their lives and simultaneously demonstrate gritty entanglements among them.

Most of the conflict has been resolved and the film is nearly over when Jackson and Travolta decide to end a harrowing and exhausting day and night with breakfast at a diner—the same diner where the movie began. They slide into a booth and place their orders a few minutes before the psychopathic couple stage their crazed and daring hold-up. The two men allow the robbery to take place while safeguarding themselves and the patrons and the story then progresses forward to a surprising and ironic point at which one of the two is shot and killed.

What I have described to you is the very basic plot outline of the film, which, for creative nonfiction, might more aptly be called the story structure or the frame.

The frame represents a way of ordering or controlling a writer's narrative so that the elements of his book, article, or essay are presented in an interesting and orderly fashion with an interlaced integrity from beginning to end.

5.2   The Chronological Story

Some frames are very complicated, as in *Pulp Fiction*, where Tarantino skillfully tangles and manipulates time. But the most basic frame is a simple beginning-to-end chronology.

For example, *Hoop Dreams*, a dramatic documentary, begins with two African American teenage basketball stars who live in a ghetto and share a dream of stardom in the NBA. The film dramatically tracks both of their careers over the next six years. The essays in the Readings section also are chronological.

Can you find the frame or story structure in the excerpts so far reprinted in this book? The story of the quitter horse on the treadmill sticks to a very basic four-scene chronology: from an introduction of Dr. Parente in his office, to the horse working out twice on the treadmill, to the final diagnosis—the resolution.

The Wendy Freeman dis-budding scene is part of a much longer essay, but it is also framed chronologically. The essay begins when she leaves her office in the early morning to go on a series of house or farm calls:

> Dr. Wendy Freeman, who is a Field Service veterinarian at New Bolton, the rural campus of the University of Pennsylvania's School of Veterinary Medicine, guns the mobile clinic pick-up truck out of the parking lot and down the road, the oversize rear tires spitting gravel.

The dis-budding scene occurs in the middle of the essay, while the essay ends when she returns to her office in the late afternoon to see a final patient and to perform a sad but unavoidable euthanasia.

Wendy Freeman stoops on a patch of grass adjacent to the parking lot near her office, examining a brown Nubian goat inflicted with a rare kidney disease far too expensive for its owner to afford to treat. The goat's owner is a woman with whom she has worked for a half-dozen years who is suffering from an increasingly debilitating case of multiple sclerosis.

The conversation is short and to the point; the woman's options are significantly limited. "Okay," she says to the veterinarian, holding her hand like a traffic policeman, palm straightforward, signalling STOP. "That's enough talk."

Looking back, I realize that the euthanasia happened quite quickly, but at the time it occurred, the process seemed agonizingly long. I watched it in kind of a 10-second delay, as if it was being played back to me in slow motion.

Wendy Freeman takes out a catheter with a long tube filled with pink liquid (sodium phenobarbital) and injects it into the goat's neck. First blood spatters onto the veterinarian's hand from the catheter. For an instant, the little goat seems to simultaneously inflate itself—and momentarily freeze—midair. Then comes a silent single shudder that ripples like quiet thunder through every dip and graceful curve of her dramatic and biblical body. Finally, the goat caves in, collapses on the grass with a muffled thud.

Now the woman cries. She sits on the ground and pets her goat, stroking the goat's ears and laying each ear, one at a time, back on top of the forehead, tears streaming down her wrinkled cheeks. Freeman reaches down and attempts to close the goat's eyes with the palms of her hands. But the eyes open back up again, continuing to assert themselves. Those eyes are ice blue. They look like diamonds or stained glass glinting in the sun.

I don't know if anyone realized what has happened at that particular moment. Or why Freeman selected such a public place to perform such a private act. Many people seemed to be going about their day as if nothing had changed, as if an animal hadn't lost a life and a woman, who herself is slowly dying, hadn't lost a friend.

On the other side of the grass, a stable hand loading a horse on a trailer is talking loudly to a companion. Maintenance workers drive by, smiling and waving. Daphne, a high school student who has been interning with Freeman, has joined us in our tight little circle of mourning. The goat continues to shudder and groan, the woman stroking its ears.

"He's already dead," the woman says aloud. "Even though he's making these noises, I know they're involuntary. He's not coming back."

Soon the woman struggles to her feet, hobbles back to the road and climbs shakily into her pick-up truck. She starts the motor and drives away. I can see her watching us in her rearview mirror. Now Daphne, the veterinarian and I are standing alone on the grass, staring quietly down at the goat. "It was a nice goat," Wendy Freeman says. "I wanted to tell the woman, 'Let's put her in the hospital and I'll pay the charges to fix her up.' It would have cost $300. But I do too much of that; I just didn't want to spend my own money this time."

5.3   Manipulating Time

A bit more complicated frame (but not as convoluted as *Pulp Fiction*) is *Forrest Gump*, which opens with Tom Hanks sitting on a bus-stop bench sharing the details of his life from birth up to this moment with any stranger willing to listen. When the viewer finally learns how Gump came to be sitting on this bench and where the bus will take him, half the film is over. The story continues chronologically when Gump boards the bus.

As demonstrated in *Pulp Fiction* and *Forrest Gump*, writers do not always frame in a strictly chronological sequence. My book, *One Children's Place*, begins in the operating room at a children's hospital, introducing a surgeon, whose name is Marc Rowe, his severely handicapped patient, Danielle, and her mother. Debbie has dedicated every waking moment to her daughter Danielle, including two years of her life spent inside the walls of this hospital with other parents from all across the world whose children's lives are too endangered to leave the confines of the hospital.

As Danielle's surgery goes forward, the reader tours the hospital in a very intimate way: observing in the Emergency Room; participating in helicopter rescue missions as part of the emergency trauma team; attending ethics meetings, well-baby clinics, child abuse examinations. The reader is taken into every conceivable activity at a typical high-acuity children's hospital, learning from the inside out how such an institution and the people it services and supports function on an hour-by-hour basis. We even learn of Marc Rowe's guilty conscience about how he has slighted his own wife and children over the years so that he can care for other families.

The book ends when Danielle is released from the hospital. I dedicated two years to researching and writing this book, returning on a day-and-night basis to Children's Hospital in order to understand the hospital and the people who made it special, but the story in which it is framed begins and ends in a few months.

Many Sleepless Nights, my book about the world of organ transplantation, begins when 15-year-old Richie Becker secretly takes his father's sports car on a joy ride. Three blocks from his home, he wraps the car around a tree and is subsequently declared brain dead at the local hospital. Devastated by the experience, but hoping for some positive outcome to such a senseless tragedy, Richie's father, Dick, donates his son's organs for transplantation.

Then the story flashes back a half century, detailing surgeons' first attempts at transplantation and all the experimentation and controversy leading up to the development and acceptance of transplant techniques.

I introduce Winkle Fulk, a mother of four, dying with an incurable heart disease, and Rebecca Treat, a recent high school graduate with hepatitis, who is in a coma and near death.

Richie Becker's liver is transplanted into Rebecca, and his heart and lungs are sewn into Mrs. Fulk. The last scene of the book is dramatic and telling and finishes the frame three years later, when Winkle Fulk travels to Charlotte, North Carolina, to personally thank Richie's father for his son's gift of life.

> At the end of the evening, just as we were about to say goodbye and return to the motel, Dick Becker stood up in the center of the living room of his house, paused, and then walked slowly and hesitantly over toward Winkle Fulk, who had once stood alone at the precipice of death. He eased himself down on his knees, took Winkle Fulk by the shoulder, and simultaneously drew her closer, as he leaned forward and placed his ear gently but firmly between her breasts, and then at her back.
>
> Everyone in that room was suddenly and silently breathless, watching as Dick Becker listened for the last time to the absolutely astounding miracle of organ transplantation: the heart and the lungs of his dead son Richie, beating faithfully and unceasingly inside this stranger's warm and loving chest.

5.4 Circular Construction

Note the circular way in which essays are constructed. *Many Sleepless Nights* begins and ends with Richie Becker; *One Children's Place* begins and ends with little Danielle; *Stuck in Time* begins and ends with Daniel. Even the essay about the treadmill begins with the concept of the quitter (a horse that quits) and ends with the repetition of the phrase along with the resolution of the problem (a partial answer to the owner's nagging question: "Why does this horse quit?") just as Quentin Tarantino chooses to begin and end (almost) in a diner.

5.5 Finding a Frame

As in many questions about writing, there is not an easy way to explain how to find a story that frames your narrative. On the surface, one might say, "Well, I'll just tell the story from beginning to end—a simple chronology." That might be a perfectly appropriate idea, but it is not so cut-and-dried.

Forrest Gump might not be nearly as effective beginning with his birth and chronicling his early years; viewers remain interested partially because they want to know why he is sitting on the bus-stop bench, just as in *Pulp Fiction*, after the first diner scene, when the crazed couple plan the hold-up, a completely unrelated story is told. But in the back of a reader's mind exists a growing curiosity about how and when the diner scene will fit in. This significantly enhances suspense.

Even if you decide that a story told in chronological order is the best and most effective idea, how does a writer know when, exactly, to begin the chronology? For "The Quitter," I actually spent a couple of days with Parente, learning about his life as an equine sports medicine surgeon. This was the sixth horse I had observed going through the treadmill diagnostic process.

The best answer to finding a frame and where in the process to start it is to isolate a point in the story at which a major action or conflict or idea resolution is about to take place. Begin a little bit before that point so that you can easily work up to it. Starting a frame or story as close to the heat of the action as possible is the best way to involve readers and compel them onward.

5.6 Classic Frames and Essential Schedules

James Baldwin's popular and fascinating autobiography of his first 21 years is framed by the funeral of his father, which is introduced on the first page and is finally concluded 53 painful and compelling pages later when his father is actually lowered into the ground.

John Wideman's *Brothers and Keepers* begins when Wideman's younger brother Robert is involved in a robbery that goes sour, panics and shoots his victim, then travels to Wyoming to touch base with his elder brother. It ends with Robert in jail a few years later. The book provides an incredible history of Wideman's family in the ghetto, of Wideman's search for respectability and escape, and an understanding of Robert's inability to follow in his brother's footsteps.

Annie Dillard's book *The Writing Life* contains an essay called "Schedules," which begins with her own musing about writing schedules for herself specifically, and writers generally.

Poet Wallace Stevens, Dillard tells us, woke up at 6:00, read for two hours, and then walked three miles to his office where he dictated poems to his secretary. He then walked home.

Jack London off and on wrote 20 hours a day. London set his alarm to wake him after four hours of sleep. "Often, he slept through the alarm," says Dillard, "so . . . he rigged it to drop a weight on his head. I cannot say that I believe this, though a novel like *The Sea Wolf* is evidence that some sort of weight fell on his head with some frequency—though you wouldn't think a man would claim credit for it."

A writer's working accommodations are usually spare, not a place to entertain or be entertained—or to be amused or distracted. On Cape Cod, where she wrote this book, Dillard worked in a prefabricated tool shed, 8 x 10 feet, the kind you buy at Hechingers or K-Mart, crammed with all of the high-tech necessities, like computer, printer, photocopying machine, air conditioner, heater and, of course, a coffee pot or kettle.

When she became too interested in the world outside her shed, she cut out squares of paper and pasted them over each pane of glass. Then, so as not to feel too boxed in, she painted realistic renditions of birds, trees, and wildflowers.

Dillard's essay ends exactly as it begins, pondering her own schedules in writing and life.

All of the essays offered in the Readings section of this book are also framed. Margaret Gibson's "Thou Shalt Not Kill" is framed chronologically around a summer visiting her family's farm and the many realities of survival in both urban and country life, such as raising animals for food.

Donald Morrill's essay contains a double frame, as does Jeanne Marie Laskas' "Garden in Winter," for they are writing parallel narratives, that is, telling two stories simultaneously and integrating them so they read as one overall narrative.

The tragic loneliness and hardship of a woman's life is relived in "Teeth," an essay about a woman who lives in the Pennsylvania backwoods. The essay is framed from beginning to end in a sequence that is perhaps in literal time—the beginning and the end of the story are only about a half hour apart.

5.7   The Eccentricities of the Writing Life

As you might have gathered by reading my description of Dillard's "The Writer's Life," writers are permitted (and usually expected) to be eccentric, exhibiting behaviors often triggered by the monklike existence they are forced to endure for hours on end, then seeking relief, finding balance.

Jack London is said to have been alcoholic and socially inept, as was Thomas Wolfe, who sometimes wrote nonstop for 36 hours, then drank whiskey and caroused through Greenwich Village until he collapsed in a stupor of exhaustion and relief. Other literary superstars then and now, F. Scott Fitzgerald, Truman Capote, and Raymond Carver included, were similarly unable to balance the isolation required by the writing and the appetite to live life to its fullest, perhaps as a relief from the cloistered writing life.

Creative nonfiction writers are permitted to be eccentric, but they must try not to be too egocentric.

John McPhee discusses his craving for relief, as well, which sometimes arrives in ways that he least wants or expects. His process of collecting information and turning it into writing begins with notes in the field. He then types those notes into an informational journal: basically unrelated, detailed entries from which he eventually works to produce a first draft.

Then, one at a time, he attaches each page of the draft to a clipboard and props the clipboard up in front of a day bed, "and then I lie down," he says, "and frequently go to sleep. I feel that that's a nervous response to the pressures of writing."

After a few minutes, he opens his eyes and starts marking this rough draft with pencil. "It is at this point that the real writing begins."

McPhee, a bearded grizzled-looking character with a gravelly voice and a self-effacing manner, discusses some of the daily habits of his work:

"I just walk around here, make a cup of coffee or tea, look out the window, inventing ways to avoid writing. Gradually through the day, some kind of pressure accumulates until 4:00 or 5:00 comes along, and it is really getting to be late, and then I'll get going. If I have a good day I might actually be writing for four hours . . . tops."

This is John McPhee's schedule, the same schedule he follows each day of his writing life, unless he is out in the field researching.

Rising early in the morning and walking to campus. Preparing a beverage. Thinking. Contemplating his life and work. Writing on a regular schedule, day after dreary, difficult, drudge-filled day, is another irreplaceable, inviolable bulwark of a writer's life.

Just as musicians practice their instruments every day, actors rehearse, basketball players shoot hoops, boxers do road work and spar—writers write.

As the short story writer Flannery O'Connor once observed, "Every morning between 9:00 a.m. and 12:00 p.m., I go to my room and sit in front of a piece of paper. Many times I just sit there with no ideas coming to me. But I know one thing. If an idea comes between 9:00 and 12:00, I am ready for it."

"A writer," said Ernest Hemingway, "is like a well. There are as many kinds of wells as there are writers. The important thing is to have good water in the well, and it is better to take a regular amount out, than to pump the well dry and wait for it to refill."

McPhee also experiences "enormous relief" upon completion of the book or essay, when he can happily pass it on to an editor at the New Yorker and move on to something else. The less accomplished writer is not so lucky.

For one thing, writers sometimes do not know exactly when a piece is finished; they just know that they cannot do any more with it. And for another thing, even if an essay or article is finished to the best of their ability, few writers really know whether they will ever see it in print.

Later, we will discuss how to maximize opportunities for publication and reward. Now, it is enough to say that all writers, rich or poor, famous or unknown, novelists and poets included, must work incredibly hard, read voraciously, write doggedly and faithfully, often in bare-bones surroundings—and always expect to feel insecure and alone. It is that bizarre state of the writing life, which is to be expected, endured, and enjoyed.

Here's an excerpt of my essay, "A Day in the Life of a Writer," from my young adult book, *Creative Nonfiction: How to Write It and Live It.**

4:30 A.M.

I wake up, brush my teeth and climb the stairs to my third-floor office, whole-wheat toast and steaming coffee in hand. I start writing.

At 6:30, I begin to search for a good stopping point. I try to find a place where I have finished a thought and started a new one and know where I am going, so that when I return to my work, I can regain lost momentum.

I go downstairs and wake up my family, listen to the news and weather report. After we breakfast together, I return to my office, usually with my 4th or 5th cup of coffee and more toast or cereal, and I write for a few more hours.

9:45 A.M.

Phase 2 kicks in at this point—toying with words—a process for which there is no trick. Sometimes it's tedious and sometimes it's fun—and it is always difficult and time-

*Excerpts from *Creative Nonfiction: How to Live It and Write It* by Lee Gutkind, © 1996. Reprinted by permission of Chicago Review Press, Inc.

consuming. You must play with your words until your sentences sing back to you. Until the words sound perfect in your head.

Here's an editor's check list for you to follow:
— Is every character and every place adequately and uniquely described?
— In these descriptions do you use descriptive ("fat" or "$10") or specific ("lean") words? You want to use specific detail only.
— Search for—and immediately destroy—cliches.
— Look for unnecessary words and "word multiples."

11:00 A.M.

After I have written 4 or 5 pages, my "creative writing" disintegrates into letter writing and other "writing business."

1 P.M.

I walk down the street to pick up my son Sam for lunch. We usually go to one of the coffee shops in our neighborhood where we share bagels, apple juice, fruit and, of course, a cookie, preferably chocolate chip.

Our favorite coffee shop, Arabica, has a balcony where I often take my laptop computer or yellow legal pad to write when I feel claustrophobic or blocked in my office at home. Most writers have an alternate place to work, just in case things don't go well on any particular day. Sometimes a change of scenery triggers a creative outburst.

I often reserve the Arabica balcony in the evenings for my classes. Sometimes my students need a change of scenery for inspiration, as well, just as I require a change of place for creative work.

2:30 P.M. or so . . .

After lunch, I say goodbye to Sam and return to my office to look at student papers. I usually write an overall evaluation of a student's work and also make suggestions for editorial changes on the manuscript.

4:00 P.M. . . *or so* . . .

Whenever my head feels like it is about to fall off, I exercise. I will run 6 miles, bike 25 miles, ski the Nordic Track for 60 minutes, or lift weights at the local club.

Main Point of Focus

6.1   *Organization by Theme*

Another way of ordering or controlling a creative nonfiction narrative
(in addition to framing)—and an essential aspect of the essay, article or
book—is the main point of focus. This—the focus—is the overall theme,
meaning, or intent of a nonfiction effort.

Whether it is an essay, an article, a book, a chapter, or a singular
scene, there should always be a main point of focus that ties the elements together. The focus can also be viewed as the message of the
writing—why the writer is writing the essay, what he or she wants the
essay to say.

Once again, let us return to the excerpts and essays so far reprinted
in this book. The humorous exchange between the dog owner and the
veterinarian Gene Solomon is focused on owner compliance. In fact,
Solomon literally states the focus in the next scene.

> For the most part, owner compliance is a norm in
> Manhattan, but on the other hand, when dogs get sick, very
> often it's because of owner noncompliance.

This is a very important message of the veterinary community
generally and Dr. Solomon specifically. An animal cannot fend for itself
in the middle of Manhattan these days. The owner must take respon-

sibility. This is a message that I, too, feel is important to emphasize. Thus, all the scenes contained in this chapter are focused on owner compliance or lack thereof. Consequently, I am remaining true to the main point of focus.

Both "The Garden in Winter" and "Thou Shalt Not Kill" focus on life-and-death themes, although the messages are very different. Jeanne Marie Laskas is examining and contrasting life, death, and maturity from the point of view of someone who is losing a very old friend—and planting and nurturing the flowers in her garden. Margaret Gibson views and confronts the challenge of growing up with the loss of an-other friend (a rabbit) through a different sort of reality. But the themes in Laskas and Gibson are consistent and serve as ways of limiting and targeting the scope of a writer's explanation. *Remember that all essays and most elements contained within essays are focused on a theme around which the narrative is structured.*

6.2 Focus Also Dictates What Not to Write About

Researching my book about veterinarians, I spent a great deal of time with Dr. Solomon. I was in the examination room when Solomon examined the dog with the poor diet, and the conversation took place as I reported it. But there were other aspects of the exchange between Solomon, the dog's owner, and the daughter that I did not report, such as a few words concerning the office's new computerized invoicing pro-cedures and a conversation about a mutual friend who was also a Solomon client.

Why not include those tidbits of conversation and gossip in the scene? I chose not to because none related to the focus of that particular chapter, which specifically concerned how Solomon interacted with his clients and how very loving animal owners can inadvertently hurt their pets.

In another scene in this chapter (called "Office Hours") I intro-duced a woman who was distressed about how tense her 10-pound terrier seemed; she wanted to take him to a salon to have him "rolfed," a method of deep, intense massage.

Solomon is aghast, not only because "rolfing" would not be a particularly pleasant experience for a terrier under the best of circumstances, but because this dog had been frequently medicated with the steroid prednisone, which weakens bones considerably. The poor puppy would be crushed. Consequently, this scene remains within the focus of this chapter. It does not relate to owner compliance, but it does have very much to do with how owners think about their pets.

On the other hand, if the main point of focus of this chapter had concerned pandemonium or disorganization in Solomon's office, then the conversation concerning the new billing system might have been focused, *if it had related to the idea of organization.*

And if the focus concerned the interrelatedness of Solomon's clients, then the conversation in the examination room relating to mutual friends might have been appropriate to recreate or report.

In "I Give Up Smiling," Donald Morrill goes off on many interesting tangents, from China, to Des Moines, to Tampa, Florida. He discusses old friends, new friends, street people, and his father. Laskas also takes us off on a number of tangents—even on a train ride with an Amish boy with a Walkman and an old lady who fell out of the train and nearly killed herself. But for both Laskas and Morrill, the theme or focus remains constant.

Ask yourself, Does this scene, story, fact, and so forth relate to my focus? If it does not, then you will probably not want to include it.

6.3   How to Sound Objective While Being Subjective

At the beginning of this book, we discussed the traditional journalist's need to be balanced and objective and the innate freedom enjoyed by the creative nonfiction writer unburdened by impossible and artificial restrictions.

I said then that in creative nonfiction, balance and objectivity are certainly permitted and sometimes desirable, but they are not required. Finding focus and remaining focused, as in this instance with Solomon and his client interactions, is a good example of how a writer can sound completely objective while actually being very subjective, by eliminating certain aspects of an interaction or experience.

Not that I misled my readers, for nothing untoward occurred. But if, for example, I would have overheard the mother and daughter saying things about Solomon that were unflattering, it would have been my choice to decide whether such information should be included in my chapter.

No such comments were made, but I would not have included them in any case—or at least not in this context—unless those comments reflected my focus. I might have included them in another chapter or a related essay having to do with how Solomon's clients related to or respected him.

6.4   *Having an Impact on—and Persuading—the Reader*

One of the primary reasons I enjoy and appreciate writing creative nonfiction is the potential ways in which I can affect my readers and directly cause change. My sincere wish is that the "Office Hours" essay will not only inform and entertain my readers, but will provide a vivid example of how a person's best intentions may not lead to the best or most desirable results. If owners are more compliant—and follow the doctor's orders—then perhaps an animal's daily lifestyle and lifespan will be more enjoyable and long lasting.

Reaching out and touching readers is what focus is all about—determining your theme or message and targeting it in a subtle but real manner.

Part 2

The Nonfiction Part

Information Transfer and the Personal Point of View

The creative aspect of the creative nonfiction experience should be utilized to make the teaching element—the nonfiction part of the product—more provocative.

7.1 This Is Not an Ego Trip

So far, we have directed our discussion at the creative part of the creative nonfiction genre: scenes (with dialogue, description, point of view, intimate detail; framing (story structure), and focus—all important aspects of the anatomy of the essay. But we have yet to discuss the most vital and irreplaceable aspect of all, the reason we are attempting to be creative: the nonfiction part of the essay. I like to call this the teaching element or the information transfer.

As editor of the only literary journal devoted exclusively to nonfiction prose, *Creative Nonfiction*, I receive approximately 150 unsolicited essays, book excerpts, and profiles a month to evaluate for possible publication. We buy only one or two of these manuscripts, however.

Of the many reasons the vast majority of these submissions are rejected, two are most prevalent. The first is an overbearing egocentrism; in other words, writers write too much about themselves without seeking a universal focus or umbrella so that readers are properly and firmly engaged. Just because something we think is interesting has happened to us, it won't necessarily be fascinating to 100,000 readers across the United States.

We all have friends who talk about themselves (and their kids, parents, employers, and so on) incessantly, and we learn when to tune them out. But when they begin to tell a story that might involve us or people we know, or make us curious about a subject or place, we tune back in. Essays that are so personal that they omit the reader are essays that will never be published. The overall objective of the personal essayist is to make the reader tune in—not tune out.

7.2   The Teaching Element

The second reason *Creative Nonfiction* and most other journals and magazines reject essays is their authors' lack of attention to the mission of the genre, which is to gather and present information, to teach readers about a person, place, idea, or situation.

Even the most personal of essays are full of substantive detail about a subject that affects or concerns a writer and the people about whom he or she is writing. Read the books and essays of the most renowned nonfiction writers of this century and you will read about a writer engaged in a quest for information and discovery.

From George Orwell in "Shooting an Elephant" to Ernest Hemingway in *Death in the Afternoon* (bullfighting) to Annie Dillard in *Pilgrim at Tinker Creek* (the natural world), along with John McPhee, Diane Ackerman, Cynthia Ozick, and George Plimpton—books and essays written by these writers are invariably about a subject other than themselves, although the narrator will be intimately included in the story.

Remember that first and foremost, you are writing for a reader. You are undoubtedly also writing for yourself, but the reader is not concerned with whether you perceive the experience with satisfaction. Rather, readers care about whether the time and effort they have invested in your writing will bear fruit. Your presence in the essay provides a personal context to a larger subject or issue.

The foundation of the creative nonfiction experience is the nonfiction—the information transfer or the teaching element. This is a three-dimensional teaching experience and not just an exercise that communicates information. The writer captures the adventure, the people behind the adventure, and the panoramic landscape of the place in which the adventure occurs. Creative nonfiction also provides the opportunity for the writer to present a very personal portrait of the experience.

7.3   *Where the Narrator Fits*

In "The Stunt Pilot," from *The Writing Life*, an in-depth and intense profile of stunt pilot Dave Rahm, Annie Dillard ruminates about her own fears and fantasies concerning flight, and she forges fascinating connections between her own struggles and triumphs as a writer and Rahm's daring artistry in the sky.

In *On Boxing*, a collection of related essays that includes a portrait of heavyweight champ Mike Tyson, Joyce Carol Oates recaptures a forgotten window of her childhood, sharing the sport of kings on Friday nights with her father.

In the essays in the Readings section of this book, Donald Morrill details and compares the neighborhoods of his life—from Iowa to Tampa to China—describes their sidewalk activities, compares their parks and trees, and recounts their changing faces, while measuring the evolution of his own life in contrast.

No one muses and measures more about her own departed world and teaches more about a lifestyle long past than Margaret Gibson in "Thou Shalt Not Kill." Gibson's scenes of childhood on a small farm in rural Virginia are skillfully intertwined by a frame and focus that revolves around killing what one loves for food.

The reader learns a great deal about Margaret Gibson's most intimate fears and feelings, but when we look up from our book at the end of the essay, we have benefited in two distinct ways: Not only have we been moved by a little girl's tragedy, but we have also learned something about how people lived—black and white, rich and poor—in a recent era.

Creative nonfiction is a dual teaching and learning experience.

7.4 To Be (The First Person Form) or Not to Be (The Third Person) . . . in the Narrative?

This is a question that most beginning writers are hungry to have answered: "Should I write my essay in the first person or the third person?"

The answer is simple: Use the voice and style with which you can most comfortably tell a story that employs scenes, dialogue, description, and the other basic tenets of creative nonfiction that we have so far discussed. More importantly, be guided by the relevancy of the "I" character.

How essential are you (the "I") to the successful dramatization of the story you are telling? If your presence is integral—if the story is enhanced by the writer becoming a part of it—then obviously, write in the first person. If, on the other hand, the writer's presence is inconsequential or worse, if the writer's presence interrupts the flow of the narrative, then obviously the third person is the preferable point of view.

Some of the most highly respected creative nonfiction writers consider the third person the more challenging point of view to master. In assessing his own work, *New Yorker* writer John McPhee once boasted about a 65,000 word book, *The Curve of Binding Energy*, in which he only used the word *I* (to refer to himself) once.

One of the triumphs of Gay Talese's "Frank Sinatra Has a Cold" essay is that the reader feels Talese's presence on every page and in every scene. However, Talese understands that he is not the subject that attracts his readers, and he has consequently chosen to profile Sinatra almost entirely in the third person. A lot of creative nonfiction is quite acceptably written in the first person. But Talese provides an essence of himself, without his literal self, which is a creative triumph.

When I was researching *Many Sleepless Nights*, I was a fly on the wall in some of the largest organ transplant centers in the world. I saw life and death played out day and night, seven days a week, month after month, for infants and old people, mothers and fathers from all over the world.

When I completed my research and sat down to write, I knew that I had witnessed some of the most vital and heart-wrenching personal dramas imaginable. Why did I need to inject myself, as long as I captured the organ transplant experience in vivid detail? Was I a recipient of a transplant? Could I vividly portray the transplant experience by just introducing my readers to the recipients and their families, friends, and surgeons? Thus, the book was written in the third person.

But I included myself in a more recent book, *Stuck in Time*, which captured the tragic and frustrating lives of children with mental health problems and their families, because I had become a mentor or big brother to one of the children about whom I was writing. As you can see, in "The Incident" (Readings) my presence was integral.

In *An Unspoken Art: Profiles of Veterinary Life*, I move in and out of the first person depending on where I am and how much I matter in any given scene or story. This is probably the best kind of compromise concerning writer point-of-view. Try not to get in the way of the narrative while maintaining a comfortable relationship with the subjects you are writing about, the story you are telling, the setting or place.

The experience is not unlike going to a cocktail party, finding a good place to stand and some nice people to chat with, moving in and out of conversations, and adjusting your participation and contribution in any given situation based on who you know in the group, how well you know (and like) them, and how much you know or are willing to reveal about the subject being discussed. Sometimes a writer can say a lot more to a reader by listening—and then responding to a conversation or situation with an overall analytical critique.

7.5   *Writing the Personal Essay*

By now you might be assuming—erroneously—that I want all writers to be journalistically oriented and not write about the conflicts and difficulties of life itself—their lives specifically. This is not true, especially if you examine the essays in the Readings section.

Tear yourself inside out. Unearth, dramatize, relive bad memories, frightening and life-shaping experiences. Tell humorous anecdotes about growing up on a farm or in the inner city. But in the process, always remember that readers have their own memories, good and bad. Readers do not want to pass the time of day with a writer, listening to the past, without learning or benefitting in one way or another—or sharing in some universal experience or agony.

Don Morrill, Margaret Gibson, and Jeanne Marie Laskas unmask themselves in the most personal ways, but they also embrace a larger subject with universal appeal.

7.6   Start a Writer's Journal

If you have not been keeping a journal or diary, it is time to start one— or a couple of them. There is a personal journal where you write your innermost feelings about life, often in a spirited, free-writing, spontaneous fashion. Then there is a writer's journal, where you record your thoughts and ideas about your writing work.

Some people use the same journal for both purposes, but then, when it comes time to consider publication, they become too reluctant to share the products of their efforts for fear of giving away too much of themselves.

In a writer's journal you conduct an ongoing, spontaneous dialogue with yourself about writing, developing the subjects and ideas you intend to or are actually writing about.

A writer's journal is honest, truthful, spontaneous, and also personal. Writers do not hold back in their personal journals; rather, they extend themselves, do the best and most vivid writing they are capable of producing.

I compare a writer's journal to an artist's sketchbook. It is where the masterpiece begins.

Begin your masterpiece. Just as an artist sketches scenes in pencil before moving into oil and canvas, record a favorite place as vividly as possible—in words.

Concentrate on all five senses: remember the smell, the taste, the sound, and the touch, as well as what you see. Listen to conversations and record the most interesting ones in a dramatic and scenic way, as if you were writing a film and not an essay—or an essay about a film you planned to write.

8

Think Globally—Act Locally

8.1   *What to Write About—I Think*

Learning how to write is hard enough, but deciding what to write about—isolating a marketable subject that is appealing to you—is the most difficult task a writer must confront. Find a subject that intrigues and motivates you and that will simultaneously intrigue and motivate readers. The task is double-edged. Salable subjects are around us everywhere; on the other hand, they are astoundingly elusive.

I remember a period of my life in the middle 1980s when I decided to move from sports-oriented books (I had traveled across the United States on a motorcycle in order to write about the motorcycle subculture, and I had observed a crew of baseball umpires for a year) to more serious subjects. I was not motivated by a special interest, such as politics or science; I simply wanted to write about something that mattered more than baseball or two-wheeled machines. For various reasons, and after a long and arduous process of research and thought, I settled upon the hostilities in Lebanon and its capital, Beirut.

At the time, there was a lull in the conflict between the Arabs and the Israelis. An area in Beirut had evolved called the green line, in which Christians and Muslims were living in peace and had established a comfortable island of commerce. According to many of the experts I consulted, the green line (literally the dividing line of a busy neighborhood) was a peninsula of peace that would soon expand into a continent of contentment—a certain sign of the turning tide.

Convinced that I had uncovered a story that needed to be told and that would affect the world, I invested many hours in library research and in conducting personal interviews with Lebanese who had fled their country. Beirut had been one of the most affluent and enlightened cities in the world at one time. Interviewing these former residents evoked fascinating images of the past and a real excitement about the potential for revitalization, with the green line as a foundation.

I went to the Lebanese consulate in Manhattan for a visa, which required a personal interview. I invested $1,200 of my own money in a roundtrip ticket to Beirut, with an extended stopover in Israel, and I boarded the plane one sunny morning—launching an odyssey that I fully expected to lead to a book.

By the time I landed in Tel Aviv 26 hours later, Israel had invaded Lebanon and the war that has actually never ended had been launched. Within hours, the green line was flooded in a river of blood. I remained in the area for a while to monitor developments with fading hopes that hostilities would end.

When I returned home, weeks later, a towering stack of mail was waiting for me on my desk—letters, bills, pamphlets, the all-too-familiar collection of junk mail that invariably would be filed in the trash can. But on top of the stack was a recent issue of *Newsweek* magazine with its lead story, "The Replaceable Body," boldly headlined. Idly, I leafed through the 12-page story and was struck by a reccurring word: Pittsburgh. It was being referred to as the organ transplant capital of the world.

This was where I lived, my hometown. The University of Pittsburgh, where all this amazing body-part replacement was taking place, was also where I taught creative writing. The medical center, in what was known as Pitt's upper campus, was a three-block uphill walk from my office in the English Department on the lower campus.

Suddenly I was struck by both the clarity and the irony of the situation: I had traveled halfway around the world to find a story that involved intense human drama and contained universal ideas and issues, when one of the most incredible stories in the history of medicine was evolving in my own backyard.

8.2   Assessing Your Informational Strengths

This is not to say that Beirut, Lebanon, and the failing possibility of peace and coexistence in the Middle East it represented, was not a good story. On the contrary, Thomas Friedman would win a Pulitzer Prize for his book, *From Jerusalem to Beirut*, less than a decade later.

But as the Middle East correspondent for *The New York Times*, Friedman was in a unique position to write such a book. Relying on the prestige of the *Times* to gain access to sources or entrée to the most private pockets of intrigue—not to mention legendary unlimited expense accounts—Friedman could unearth information and gain insights that would have easily eluded a freelancer with few connections and meager resources. Others could have written Tom Friedman's story, of course (there have been many high-quality books about the strife and frustration of the Middle East), but not me, I realized in retrospect.

But I had the edge on Tom Friedman, *The New York Times*, and any other writer I knew on the inside track toward the incredible organ transplant story. Of course, it was not a story that would generate regular front page headlines in the *Times* and continuous coverage on *ABC World News Tonight* with Peter Jennings. But it was my story—or at least it came to be mine—and it was jam packed with human life-and-death drama, with heroic figures (surgeons and patients), incredible technology, and spectacular appeal.

The discovery of this subject, which actually led to five related books and many articles and essays, taught me the unforgettable lesson that I try to impart to students and writers, wherever I go, who are seeking viable topics to capture and write about:

Think globally, act locally. A writer could live a whole life and gain international renown (and some have) without wandering so much as a mile from his or her home.

I am not recommending such an isolated and uninspiring lifestyle. On the contrary; writers must explore other places and invariably will benefit from other customs and cultures. But unless resources are free-flowing and time is of no real concern, then the most efficient way of living the writing life is selecting projects for which the foundation can be established close to home.

Many Sleepless Nights took me to England, Ireland, Australia, and all across the United States; it was not a culturally isolating experience. But by focusing it in Pittsburgh, the organ transplant capital of the world, I could also sleep in my own bed, maintain a relationship with my family, and save precious resources (time and money) in the process.

8.3 The Ideal Story Idea

The ideal story will have a potential focus located in your own backyard, but simultaneously will contain national appeal and relevance.

This is an important and ongoing distinction. When students tell me about something interesting taking place in the Pittsburgh Public School system or in their own neighborhoods, I ask the obvious and all-important question: What does this mean to the people in Cleveland, Ohio, or Salt Lake City, Utah?

To put it another way, why should the readers of *The New Yorker* or *Sports Illustrated* or any prominent magazine care one way or another about what is happening in Pittsburgh or about an interesting character in the house next door?

If you can answer the question by saying, "My neighbor trained the last three table tennis champions of the United States" or "The Pittsburgh public school system is launching an Internet network that will allow high school students to dialogue with college and university presidents across the United States," then I will say, "You have a story to tell."

If you cannot answer the question by making a global or universal connection, then keep looking.

8.4 Amassing Clippings

I am not advising beginning writers to ignore local newspapers and city magazines. Everyone is an apprentice or student somewhere for a part of his or her life. In the professional baseball world, the minor leagues provide young ballplayers with ways to hone their skills and build reputations. Those musicians who aspire to or have achieved symphony-orchestra status will have struggled through countless high school recitals and small-town performances. So it goes with writers.

Editors at major magazines, such as *The New Yorker* or *Harper's*, probably will want to know writers personally or be familiar with their work before assigning them essays or articles. If they like your idea but they do not know your writing, they will ask for samples. *Clippings* is the term used in the newspaper business; reporters are expected to have amassed a *clipbook*.

By all means, use local connections to practice writing, to become more sophisticated, and to collect a representative body of samples. But continue to try to choose subjects that do not permit you to practice provincialism. Reach out from home—wherever home is—and touch the world.

8.5   Literary Journals

For reasons discussed in the first part of this book involving a need for formulaic objectivity, the more personal the essay, the less likely your local newspaper will be interested in publishing or assigning it. In addition, because newspapers traditionally are cramped for space, long prose pieces are anathema to them.

Literary journals seek out new, high-quality writers willing to speak out about controversial subjects or detail their own difficulties navigating the complicated web of life. And literary journal editors usually abhor brevity for brevity's sake: They seek writers willing to probe a subject or psyche with meticulous care and enlightening persistence.

Literary journals are also closely monitored by literary agents and magazine and book publishers seeking superior new talent. Not long ago, *Creative Nonfiction* published an essay by a young writer who had been published by two or three other journals. A prominent literary agent in Manhattan contacted the writer about representation. Did she have enough essays for a collection, the agent wanted to know. A few months later, the agent arranged for a book contract for this writer with a major international publisher—a contract worth nearly half a million dollars.

This is a dream come true, though certainly not a frequent occurrence. It is important to remember, however, that writers will not be discovered in local newspapers or city magazines. Unless they live in Manhattan, Boston, Chicago, or San Francisco, major metropolitan areas with a strong writing and publishing community, they must reach past their hometowns and tap deep into the rhythm of the world.

Interestingly, a literary journal's circulation can be quite small—under 1,000 readers per issue is not uncommon. But most journals are published like paperback books, perfect bound with heavy coated covers, to last. They are often reprinted or overprinted so that your essay is available to readers, for purchase, for many years. Literary journals are usually quarterlies or published only semiannually, which means that the writer remains current and in print for months. Contrast this with writers who appear in *The New Yorker* or the *New York Times Magazine*, which, as one frequent contributor to both magazines told me, "end up in a week as bird-cage liner."

Another important fact to consider is that by publishing in literary journals you are often in the company of the most prestigious writers in the world. Many writers use journals as a place to experiment with new voices or controversial ideas that traditional consumer magazines would categorically reject.

Leafing through essay collections in libraries or book stores, including Robert Atwan's *Best American Essays*, consult the title page to determine where most of the work originally appeared. Three names you will recognize will be *The Atlantic Monthly*, *Harper's*, and *The New Yorker*, but the vast majority of the remaining selections will come from journals few people could recognize: *Creative Nonfiction*, *Tikkun*, *Prairie Schooner*, *The Georgia Review*, *Triquarterly*, *Granta*, *Grand Street*, and others. Hundreds of journals, many attached to universities, are published in the United States.

Most popular magazines will also avoid long essays—more than 3,000 words or approximately a dozen typewritten pages. But length is not a problem for literary magazines. Prestigious writers who have written meticulously detailed work of twice that length or more are frequently published by literary magazines.

A well-known writer, author of a dozen novels and nonfiction books, recently wrote to *Creative Nonfiction* to explain in detail how *National Geographic* had assigned him a long essay on Boston, and had paid him a great deal of money for it, but had then decided not to publish it. *Geographic* returned rights to the essay to the author, who submitted it to a smaller magazine. That magazine responded favorably to the essay, but wanted to publish a shortened version. The author balked—he wanted his 6,000-word piece published the way in which it was written—and so he contacted me.

Creative Nonfiction plans to publish the essay. A recent issue of *Creative Nonfiction* also contained an experimental self-interview by the novelist and editor Gordon Lish, which was rejected after being assigned by *Interview Magazine* because of its controversial and experimental nature.

8.6   Coping with Rejection

Creative Nonfiction and other literary journals regularly publish rejects from popular magazines, writing that may well reflect an author's best work. In this case, the writer was assigned an essay, and he completed the job within all the contractual limits, such as length, deadline, and so forth. But an editor assigning a creative effort by a creative writer is always taking a chance that the end product, although perfectly acceptable on a literary level, will not be embraced by a magazine's universal readership. The editor and the magazine are obliged to pay the writer but not to publish what has been purchased.

I suffered through a similar experience not long ago, when *The New Yorker* assigned an article ("fact piece" is what they usually call it) about the ethics of using animal organs for human transplants. (This was soon after a baboon's liver was transplanted into a man dying of AIDS.) I worked very hard on this fact piece, which was accepted with great praise and enthusiasm, and I was paid quite handsomely.

During the six months consumed in research and writing, a new editor began changing the editorial policy of the magazine—and eliminating long, serious fact pieces about science, especially if they were not newsworthy. The baboon transplant had not been attempted again. *The New Yorker* kept the article for 18 months and then returned it to me. I revised it and resubmitted it to *The Atlantic*, which immediately purchased it. Thus, I was paid a second time for the same work—not so handsomely, but reasonably.

However, my animal organ fact piece has never been published. *The Atlantic* scheduled it three times—and changed its mind each time because other medically oriented stories have conflicted. Eventually, the information presented in the article and the ideas I articulated were no longer unique.

The point is that writers cannot be evaluated completely by the prominence of the magazines in which their work appears. Many factors other than writers' talent enter into the magazine's decision to publish their work, including timing and editorial preference. The publishing world is fickle, as are the leaders of the publishing industry, who switch allegiance from magazine to magazine and make radical changes to the products they edit. If a writer is caught in the crossfire, so be it.

I am not recommending that writers ignore rejection, because that would be an impossible and unwise suggestion. But before becoming depressed or angry, try to analyze the reasons for rejection, when possible. It might have nothing to do with your work.

Of course, you may not know the reason you are being rejected, because form letters have become the normal way in which magazine editors respond to writers. But receiving many form letters is an important signal that is not to be ignored. Most editors I know, myself included, go out of their way to discover or encourage emerging talent by writing personal letters of rejection or personal notes on the rejection form itself when they read a work with merit—work that comes really close to being accepted.

If your work is regularly rejected with form letters, you may not necessarily judge yourself to be a poor writer, but it is fair to say that you may not yet be good enough to deserve the attention of a harried editor, pressed for time. It is a signal for you to heed.

Make certain that you are submitting essays and ideas to the right magazines. You probably will not sell an article about football, for example, to *Cosmopolitan*. Do you read the magazines to which you submit work to make certain the content, style, and length are appropriate? It is surprising to discover how many writers submit essays to *Creative Nonfiction* without having the slightest idea what the genre is all about.

Reexamine the basic principles of the anatomy of an essay as outlined in the first part of this book. Be certain that you are writing scenically and that information (the teaching element) is prominent. Finally, downsize your dreams, at least for the moment. To some writers, *The New Yorker* is the Carnegie Hall of the essay-writing world. Remember that it takes a while to reach the pinnacle of a career—in fact, for a myriad of reasons many very successful classical musicians will never play in Carnegie Hall—and there is no reason to be in any hurry to get there.

Besides, as both musicians and writers (and various other artists) will tell you, there are a great many compromises required to get to the top. Along the way, you can lose your connection to or vision of the work itself. Is it better to be published where most people can acknowledge your work? Or, conversely, is it better to have a smaller audience for the best work you can write? This is not always a compromise writers are forced to make, but it is one they should anticipate.

8.7   Agents and Editors

Editors will nurture writers who have talent because good writers make their jobs easier. After all, an editor's primary responsibility is to fill up the magazines or sections of magazines for which they are responsible with the best work possible. The writers they attract and the issues that they edit are similar to clippings—examples of what they can do.

However, editors are gypsies. They move from job to job frequently. That is the nature of the publishing business. What happens to the writer in the process of these career moves is never clear to predict. When editors go to magazines similar to those they have left, it is good for their writers. But what happens to the work they have purchased for their original magazines—your essay or profile—is up in the air. New editors will have their own vision to put on the magazine, and if the backlog of essays and articles collected by the original editors do not fit in with this vision, they will not be used.

In book publishing, frequently editors lobby the editorial board for authors with whom they want to work on intriguing ideas. When it comes time for books to be considered for marketing and advertising funds, editors are supposed to champion their authors' cause.

But what if an editor has moved on to another position? It is possible that the editor's new company will purchase the writer's contract, but this does not happen frequently. It is more likely that another editor will be assigned to the project—a person with little or no commitment to the project or the writer. Many writers, including the most prominent, will have an abandonment story to tell, a situation in which they suddenly found themselves in literary limbo.

Is this the moment for your literary agent to step in and take control of the situation? It probably is, but that does not usually happen. Writers expect too much from their agents; agents are not unlike real-estate salespeople who benefit by maintaining strong relationships with both parties in the negotiation, editors and writers, buyers and sellers.

Although it is true that an agent will only make money by taking a percentage of the commissions of what the writers they represent sell, it behooves them not to alienate editors and publishers, because they have other clients to represent. There might be a half-dozen additional negotiations with that same editor (and other writers) in any given year. The writer often leans too much on the agent and frequently is disappointed with the results.

Then what should a writer expect from a good agent? An agent should know many editors and be able to connect his or her writers to editors with similar ideas and temperaments. An agent should have an intimate knowledge of the legalities of the publishing world—contracts, rights, and so forth. A writer need not have a lawyer to examine contractual relationships with publishers; that is an agent's job. In my experience, agents know more about the narrow confines of literary law than most attorneys, unless it is the attorney's legal specialty.

How can you get an agent? Usually, a good agent will find writers and recruit them. Most agents have no interest in involving themselves in magazine work; their main interest is in books. If you have a good book idea, or if you have a book manuscript and you have not been contacted by an agent who has seen your work in print or with whom you have some sort of mutual connection, consider contacting the Association of Authors Representatives, Inc. (10 Astor Place, 3rd floor, New York, NY 10003) for a list of authorized agents.

Getting Started

9.1 *Where to Look for a Topic*

In searching for a topic for a book, article, or essay, begin in the most obvious places. Look around you, where you live, work, or attend school. Who are your neighbors and what do they do for a living? Any interesting people or professions on your block or in your apartment building? What stories are hidden in your neighborhood?

Within walking distance of my house, for example, there are six coffee shops that have opened in the past three years, each doing a booming business. Here in the 1990s, in a climate hostile to the small independent business person, there seems to be life and profit in fancy, expensive coffee and conversation.

What does this mean to the business community locally and nationally? Are bars and cocktail lounges becoming less appealing to the night-time crowd? Is urban America becoming increasingly more European in temperament and personality? How is it that book stores and coffee shops came to work together, as in the Barnes and Noble and Starbucks nationwide alliance? Again, I ask one of the vital questions: What does this mean?

Interspersed between the coffee shops are three bagel bakeries. Think of this: Bagels have become a popular snack food. Everyone suddenly seems to be eating bagels. You can buy pizza bagels, Mexican bagels, green bagels on St. Patrick's Day. Bagel shops proliferate in rural areas.

But who invented the bagel? Why are they suddenly in such vogue? How are they baked . . . or cooked . . . or fried?

Around the corner from where I live, there is a police and fire station. I could pass the time of day with the people who work there, learn their names and schedules. Gradually, I would begin to understand the intimate rhythm of the place and the personalities of the people who make that place special.

If true-life police dramas are so popular and effective on TV or as feature films, then why not books, articles, and essays? The highly respected police drama, *Homicide: Life on the Streets*, filmed on location in Baltimore and produced and directed by Barry Levinson (*Diner*), was actually adapted from a book of the same name, published in 1990.

If you live in an area where there is a college or university, then there are undoubtedly enough ideas for articles and essays to support you for a year—or perhaps for the rest of your life. Academics represent an absolute catalog of creative ideas and accomplishments (not to mention fascinating failures).

My medically oriented books were national in scope, published by national publishers and reviewed in major newspapers across the United States. Collectively, they have appeared in five languages.

Comb the campus of your choice, wherever you live. There are architects, engineers, philosophers, political scientists (and pundits), economists, athletes in a plethora of sports, and a range of personalities and opinions on some of the most bizarre (as well as fascinating and moving) topics imaginable.

Although entire stories will not necessarily be researched and written just by familiarizing yourself with the local institution of learning, there will be gems of ideas there.

9.2 The Dual Objective: Writing for Yourself—and Others

Subjects or ideas to develop into books, articles, and essays begin with your potential reader; you want to choose something interesting and appealing to your audience—and satisfying for you to invest your time and effort.

This latter point, personal satisfaction, is essential. Writers are not machines, or at least they should try to avoid producing prose on demand. Sometimes, because of financial pressures, we are forced to write about subjects in which we have little interest. There are bills to pay and children to feed. But whenever possible, writers should attempt to satisfy the dual objective of making a living while enjoying their work. This often requires a certain subtle compromise and a reorientation of how to view traditional subjects.

As I have said, many of my books have been medically oriented: organ transplantation, pediatrics, psychiatry, veterinary life. Aware of my ambivalence to science generally and physicians specifically, friends have been surprised at my choice of subjects. I'm the guy whose first books and essays required me to hang out with motorcyclists, baseball umpires, mountain men, transcontinental truck drivers—loners, basically, forgotten heroes.

But health-care issues were in the news, on the lips of politicians, business people, reporters, and consumers, and my traditional forgotten-hero theme, although interesting, limited the appeal of my work. The challenge was in making subjects I was less than enamored with into a worthwhile writing experience: Try to visualize subjects in ways that will appeal to your interests and writing strengths.

Organ transplantation may be scientific, but it is also intensely dramatic. Here are ordinary people, just like my readers, suddenly finding themselves on the absolute edge of death, subjecting themselves to the most devastating surgical experience in the history of modern medicine.

The more I considered and observed them, the more I came to realize that my concept of heroism had been skewed or was at the very least due for a readjustment. Weren't these people—I began calling them "patient pioneers"—actually more heroic and alone than those forgotten heroes about whom I had been writing?

Many of the patients I had been meeting were from other parts of the country or the world. They had been forced to leave behind family and friends and had been injected into a sterile, cold milieu where their lives were in constant jeopardy.

Truck drivers, baseball umpires, motorcyclists were interesting because of how they chose to live and work. Organ transplant candidates and recipients had no such choice: They were facing the ultimate battle of survival caused by situations (sickness, disease) over which they had little control.

Writing about people involved in the transplant experience did not absolve me of the responsibilities of writing about medical science and the physicians who make medical miracles possible, but it offered a way to help accomplish my own literary objective, which is to continually attempt to capture and understand the human experience under pressure or in an alienated situation (forgotten heroes), and to reach out and make an impact on the largest readership possible. Choosing ideas for articles and essays must accomplish the dual objective of satisfying readers and the writer's needs and desires.

For more personal essays describing life's challenges and dilemmas, begin with what you know best, like running, or basketball, or crossword puzzles, or cooking—a subject and activity with which you feel comfortable.

Start by describing one aspect of that subject, a part that you do extraordinarily well or that makes you feel good, like stirring, tasting, and seasoning simmering soup, if cooking is your passion. Ask yourself: Why does this singular act produce such satisfaction? What quality or facet of my life does it enhance or reflect? Or, conversely, what aspect does it replace?

Allow your writing to be spontaneous. Take off in as many directions as necessary, as long as each direction tells a story or paints a picture and teaches or informs at the same time.

9.3   Keeping Current

Reading what is being published today is just as essential as reading yesterday's classics.

I am not only talking about books, articles, and essays, but selected newspapers as well. Remember that writing is a business, and most business people need to know what competitors are doing and what customers (publishers and editors) are buying. In fact, nonfiction writing is more of a business than poetry or fiction writing because the product the nonfiction writer is selling is often associated with subjects or incidents related to current events.

Editors lose interest when the event is no longer newsworthy or relevant; knowing what has already been written about a subject or in a field by reading books and magazines saves a writer time and trouble.

Some subjects are worth only one burst of attention. For example, I recently read an interesting narrative in *Vogue* called "Inconceivable Conception," about the romance of Pam and Manny, and Manny's sudden and tragic death in an auto accident soon after their marriage.

Stunned and sick with grief, but dedicated to their dream of having a family, Pam immediately approached a fertility doctor who, hours after the death, successfully harvested and preserved Manny's sperm for artificial insemination. This is a scientific precedent; it has happened only once before—15 years ago—and it might not happen for another 15 years, if ever.

You may find this fascinating or disgusting; whichever, the story is thought-provoking. But unless Pam's desperate last-ditch attempt to preserve a part of her husband's memory becomes a trend, one story is enough. On the other hand, there is a large market for articles and essays that confront and discuss infertility, and the problems and issues the subject brings forth for examination and debate.

If you have an interest in writing for women's magazines or writing about women's health issues, you should familiarize yourself with *Vogue*, *Redbook*, *Cosmopolitan*, and other similar publications, so that you understand the content and quality of the stories being published.

You might also read general interest magazines such as *Vanity Fair* or *The Atlantic*, and even a few more specialized publications such as *The New England Journal of Medicine* and *JAMA* (*Journal of the American Medical Association*).

Understand the distinction: Read women's and general-interest magazines to learn what is being covered, how, and by whom, and then read *JAMA* to understand what has not yet been covered: What issues, ideas, studies, and reports might be important to explain or discuss.

Reading these latter journals may also lead to terrific story ideas that might not otherwise ever make the news. Over the past few years, for example, there has been an increasing amount of interest in Munchausen's Syndrome, a phenomenon in which mothers will stage a serious health crisis concerning their child, in which they serve in an heroic, lifesaving capacity. This sudden attention to Munchausen's, as evidenced by newspaper and magazine articles and TV movies, was initiated by a case study published in a medical journal and then rewritten for public consumption.

Even if a writer already has an idea or assignment to pursue—book, essay, or article—it is important to read everything written about your subject. Not only will you know what not to write (what other people have written), but such reading will constantly provide new ideas and perspectives with which you may view your article, along with sources you might not have considered or even known about.

A similar philosophy or approach is in effect if you are interested in sports. You would read *Sports Illustrated* or *The Sporting News*, and if politics is your bailiwick, then there's *The New Republic*, *The American Spectator*, and *The Nation*. For business, *The Wall Street Journal*, *Business Week*.

When you decide upon a specific subject about which to write, visit your local library and do a database search through the newspaper and magazine indexes. More specialized databases are also widely available. Many people can access information banks from home with a modem and their personal computer. These days it is much easier to research thoroughly and have much more fun than ever before.

Remember that the foundation of the writing life is reading: We read the best writers to understand how far we must reach toward excellence and how hard we must try. We read what is being written in our field today to keep up with our competition and to keep current on the subjects that appeal to us.

9.4   *Reading the* New York Times

Read the *New York Times* on a regular basis.

Most professional writers allow at least an hour a day to commune with the *Times*, the best way to keep apprised of what is happening nationally and internationally and in New York.

But you live in Richmond, Virginia, or Bellingham, Washington. Why read the *New York Times?* Because the *Times* does what its banner proclaims, which is to publish "All the News That's Fit to Print."

Nonfiction writers must attempt to be renaissance intellectuals, tuning in to the events that shape history, as well as the less important aspects of the news that the *Times* records daily.

And the *Times Sunday Book Review* offers an overview of the most popular books in print. On Mondays, the *Times* business section focuses on media.

Most writers have what might be termed a "futures" file—a list of ideas or newspaper clippings for essays or articles they might someday want to write. The vast majority of my futures file clippings comes from scouring the *Times*.

Why did I clip these stories, other than the fact that I was intellectually interested? Because each story I clipped took place in my hometown, which is a key element in the kind of stories we should try to develop: A local landscape with a *New York Times*-anointed global significance.

9.5   *Research Before Writing*

Previously, in a tour of my neighborhood, seeking ideas for articles and essays, we came across three bagel bakeries, six coffee shops, and a nearby police station. There is also a golf course (how many golf courses can you think of located in a major metropolitan area?), a rehabilitation institute for handicapped children, and a large and continuously expanding orthodox Jewish community. These are all interesting potential stories with the possibility of national relevance and impact, perfectly in line with the concept of thinking globally and acting locally.

Whether you are writing traditional or creative nonfiction, there are three ways to research these or any other potential essay, book, or article idea: Begin with library research, then interview the most important people, then allow yourself a personal experience by immersing yourself in the place or experience about which you are writing.

Technically, you could begin a writing project with any of these approaches. You could be a golfer, for example, who begins to think about the unique privilege of playing at a course two minutes from your house without having to move to the suburbs. Or you could find yourself in a conversation with a neighbor who happens to own one of those bagel bakeries, or you could see an item in your local paper that triggers your curiosity.

However you enter into a subject, I recommend that you proceed by fulfilling the easiest but the most boring task first, library research.

9.6   Assessing the Competition

My students regularly resist the library-first approach, but it is the logical first step for a number of reasons. A writer must know what the competition has done, which means researching other articles and essays that have been published. You would be foolish to invest in a new ice cream parlor in a shopping mall when Baskin-Robbins and Häagen Dazs franchises are already in place.

From a writer's point of view, if your idea is good, then someone is likely to have written it. This does not mean that you have lost your idea if you do discover articles about bagels or police stations. It means that you must find an angle or approach—*a main point of focus*—that is significantly new and different to make the end product salable.

Researching first will save time and trouble, and it may also provide insight into the unique theme or focus you are seeking. I devoted a couple of weeks to library research and reading for my book, *Stuck in Time*, about children with serious mental-health problems. I had initially conceived this book as an examination of the technological and biological advances into the causes of mental-health problems made in an era the National Institutes of Health called "The Decade of the Brain."

But after familiarizing myself with the available literature, I discovered that this new era in "brain-biology" research was a figment of the NIMH's imagination and a publicity gimmick; very little substantive work had been written about "the decade of the brain" because it did not exist. Although the fact that "the decade of the brain" was a governmental sham was in itself a good article or essay idea, it was not enough for a book, which was what I was attempting to develop.

By the same token, I discovered that treatment of children with mental-health problems was often based upon clinical research conducted on adults, although psychiatrists were quick to admit that children reacted differently to medication than adults. Most articles and books about mental-health problems were written by psychologists or psychiatrists. Few were authored by patients or victims of mental illness, and fewer still were conceived by the most victimized subgroup of all—the families (parents, siblings, children) of people who suffered from such diseases as manic depression or schizophrenia.

I noticed this family gap in the social-support structure while writing two other books about health care. For the organ transplant experience in *Many Sleepless Nights*, the health-care system was structured to counsel patients but not the people who were often responsible for the patients or who were forced to deal with the side effects of serious illness of a family member. Wives of bedridden husbands must often, quite suddenly, become breadwinners and father figures to their children, and when a mother is concerned with a dying husband and mounting debts, her children often are left to dangle in isolation and neglect with relatives far from home.

In the process of learning that the book I had initially intended to write could not be written, I was able to shape and focus an idea for a book that had never been written but one that could address an open audience with a real need for attention and explanation.

Admittedly, this process of digesting and understanding the issues while reading articles and book chapters in the library was not as clear to me then as it was two years later, when my book was researched, written, and ready for publication, because I needed to fulfill my researching agenda by asking many questions of a number of experts in the field, not to mention patients and family members themselves. In addition, I needed to immerse myself in the world of mental health in a number of different situations and milieus. The seeds and suspicions that led to my main points of focus, however, took root in the library during those initial weeks.

9.7   Thinking Is an Integral Part of Writing

There are two additional points to ponder in relation to the researching and writing process. Previously, I discussed the traditional journalist's role as a reporter committed to communicating the facts behind a person, place, or situation, rather than the insight or rationale behind the facts. But the essayist—the creative nonfiction writer—must also be a thinker, a critic, and a social commentator. My research enabled me to learn the facts of the pediatric mental-health world and then to dig down deeply behind the facts, to isolate the reasons for the gaps in the system, and to present concrete and intelligent suggestions to remedy those weaknesses. This is the coveted privilege of the essayist—to go beyond the realm of traditional reportage in order to provide a three-dimensional approach for readers.

9.8   The Trend Toward Specialization

Notice also how I relied on my experience in health care both in the organ transplant world and in pediatrics in *One Children's Place* to understand the issues and to make connections and conclusions about the problems and solutions in mental health.

Book and article editors are much more receptive to writers who have a specialization, such as health care, business and economics, or women's issues. You may have an aversion to specialization—part of the fun of being a writer is having a variety of learning experiences—but these days specialization is an economic practicality. Writers, especially those without too many prestigious credits, are more likely to receive assignments, contracts, and money if they can boast a unique expertise.

During my career, I have attempted to establish a range of related specialties: sports, nature or out-of-doors, health care, and writing (creative nonfiction), a combination that allows me to benefit from my expertise while permitting a rich variety of experiences.

A final and important reason to conduct library research first is to be able to present yourself to the people you are planning to interview as a knowledgeable writer, someone whom they can trust. Whatever the subject—bagels, nuclear medicine, or high finance—a writer should have some basic understanding of the essential issues and of the men and women in leadership positions.

If you were a coach or player in the National Football League, for example, and a reporter who came to interview you and who wanted to spend time with you did not recognize names like Dan Marino or Troy Aikman, your level of trust and your willingness to cooperate would be very low. You would not want to be investing your valuable time describing and defining Dan Marino's career to that reporter. Subjects about whom you intend to write will be impressed with your background knowledge and, therefore, will be more eager to work with you and provide you unique access to their private worlds.

9.9   Managing the Research Librarian

Librarians are trained to help constituencies on two opposite extremes: Scholars seeking an in-depth examination of a subject and consumers interested in tracking down arcane facts or confirming basic ideas and principles, such as the birthplace of Andy Warhol (Pittsburgh) or the location of an area well known in the publishing world called Printer's Row (Chicago). A writer's needs, especially in this initial stage of the research, fall in between those extremes.

You do not have a few facts to unearth or confirm; you may not have any facts at all. Your interest may be based on an article you clipped from a newspaper or magazine or on a conversation you overheard on a bus. Librarians like to lead people who expect more information toward the academic indexes and archives, a potential destination for a writer deeply engaged in research, but not at this stage of the journey.

A writer must carefully guide the librarian to concentrate on databases and indexes that will satisfy a need to understand the basics of the subject and to assess the competition—essentially to find out what others have written, while isolating the names and locations of the movers and shakers in the field and being introduced to the general ideas and concepts of the area of interest.

The best places to gain this information are the various magazines and newspaper indexes, which will access the *New York Times, The Wall Street Journal, Newsweek,* and *Time.* There are literally dozens of these general indexes, providing citations and a paragraph-long description of the contents. Some libraries offer sophisticated computer equipment, which allows you to print out the entire article. You can also do this work at home through use of the World Wide Web.

Immersion

10.1 Access to the Inside

In creative nonfiction, access and immersion are the operative words.

For *Many Sleepless Nights*, I was eventually permitted to enter into the organ transplant operating rooms with complete freedom, to jet through the night on organ donor harvests, to roam the hospital corridors, to accompany the surgeons on rounds, and to attend ethics committee meetings and social service consults at will.

For *Stuck in Time*, I possessed a master key to all units in one of the largest psychiatric hospitals in the country, and I sat in as a silent observer in family therapy between an adolescent child suffering from manic depression, her mother and father, and a prominent child psychiatrist. Key scenes and dramatic confrontations in these books occurred during these periods of privacy and intimacy, which are pretty much unavailable to the traditional reporter.

Although the access I have achieved behind previously closed doors is quite special, it is not that rare for experienced creative nonfiction writers, especially those who specialize in what is often called immersion journalism. Tracy Kidder and John McPhee have forged their leading reputations in the immersion journalism field because of their willingness to invest the time necessary to literally immerse themselves in a new and different way of life for prolonged periods.

In a career spanning three decades and with more than 25 published books, John McPhee has lived as a journalist/observer as no one else has. *The John McPhee Reader* introduces excerpts from a variety of McPhee classic immersion experiences, including *The Survival of the Birch Bark Canoe*, in which McPhee embarks on a canoe trip with Henri Vaillancourt, a superb craftsman who, McPhee ironically discovers, is an egocentric novice as a canoe voyageur; a book-length profile of Bill Bradley, the NBA superstar who soon went on to represent New Jersey in the United States Senate; *Levels of the Game*, an in-depth examination of tennis, framed in the context of one match; and *Oranges*, which might be subtitled "Everything you never imagined but found fascinating to learn about a favorite fruit."

Tracy Kidder seems to specialize in year-in-the-life experiences, from inside a nursing home, to an elementary school classroom, to what is often described as his best book, *House*, tracking the design and construction of a house from the varied and intimate point of view of the participants: architect, owner, carpenter, and contractor.

Whereas McPhee seeks out more exotic and far-afield subjects for his work, Kidder is especially skillful in practicing the dictum of think globally act locally, selecting the most common and ordinary life experiences affecting millions of Americans, all researched and written in his native New England and within driving distance of his home.

Immersion is a fairly new way to describe this in-depth personal aspect of the researching experience, although it has been around for a long time. Published in the 1960s, George Plimpton's *Paper Lion*, in which the author trains with the Detroit Lions of the NFL, is immersion journalism. Ernest Hemingway, winner of the Nobel Prize in Literature, first made his mark as a newspaper reporter. During his distinguished career, he wrote three creative nonfiction books: *The Green Hills of Africa*, *A Moveable Feast* (a memoir) and his unforgettable paean to bull fighting, *Death in the Afternoon*.

Hemingway was also a frontline correspondent for *Esquire* magazine and the North American Newspaper Alliance during World War II. Both as a novelist and as a journalist, Hemingway knew where the action was and sought to be in the thick of it whenever possible. *New Yorker* writer Lillian Ross immersed herself with Hemingway and his wife, Mary, day and night during a week in which the Nobel laureate visited New York, capturing "Papa" in his most revealing, quirky, and eccentric performance. It is a useful and amusing essay.

10.2   The Writer as the Interloper

A common misconception about access and immersion is that the writer is an interloper and a burden to the people about whom he or she is writing. Writers are often reluctant to ask for continuing access or special favors for fear of imposing.

The writer may or may not turn out to be an enduring friend, and also may or may not be imposing, but most immersion practitioners agree that they often become a welcome diversion to the people they write about in books, essays, and profiles. About asking for special favors, in my experience the challenge is access—just getting inside a place. The special favors, such as permission to enter the operating arena, usually will be forthcoming as you become a fixture in the place, trusted and unobtrusive.

Indeed, I never asked for access to transplant surgery. After about a year, I was invited and subsequently encouraged. Outfitted in scrubs, mask, paper cap, and booties, I probably observed 300 organ transplant procedures and could have observed 900 more. In retrospect, I realize that if someone would have thought more carefully about my presence, more specific rules and boundaries might have been established. But because I did not ask for special privileges and because I never got in the way or was in any way intrusive, such boundaries were never raised.

10.3   Hanging In

The secret of successful immersion is longevity. As I said, Tracy Kidder has been willing to immerse himself for a year and more in a project; this does not include the research and other preparatory work and the year or years it takes to write the book after the immersion is completed.

I began my immersion experience in the transplant world by spending time with patients and families during rounds. In that way, I became a recognizable presence to surgeons and nurses until I could eventually join them as they moved from patient to patient. This process took, off and on, about a year.

As soon as one surgeon invited me to observe surgery, most of the others followed suit. Sometimes I would use my temporary opening into the surgical world as a wedge: "Now that I have seen Dr. So-and-So do a liver transplant, do you mind if I study your techniques?" "I've already witnessed a kidney being transplanted, how about if I observe your upcoming heart transplant surgery?"

10.4 Good Immersion Writers Are Neither Seen Nor Heard

Despite the privileges you may receive as a writer and observer, the concept of becoming and remaining unobtrusive is very important. Remember that you do not want to be an imposition, and you are definitely not part of the team. The tendency is to find a place for yourself and to help out in order to make yourself be and feel useful. This approach does not usually work well.

As a writer you have as much of a job to do as the people about whom you are writing. It may not seem as if you are working, but for a writer sitting, watching, and taking the occasional note is a key and vital activity. If you are helping the people you are observing on a regular basis then you are not writing. If you are perceived as part of the team, then you are not perceived as a writer, a misconception that may lead to misunderstandings down the line, after the essay or book is published.

Besides, you have been given access because of a special project that you have proposed; people expect that you will act in a "writerly" way, whatever that is, rather than as a laborer or technician. This is not to say that you cannot participate in an experience or try out certain things that your subjects do, but usually not on a regular basis. For example, I once gave a rectal examination to a milk cow, perhaps the most intimate immersion of my career.

While immersing myself in a writing project, however, I routinely like to compare myself to a rather undistinguished and utilitarian end table in a living room or office. It is a fixture. You walk in and out of your living room dozens of times a day. You see the table, you *expect* to see the table, but you do not say, "Well, there is the table, hello table." If, on the other hand, you walk into the living room or office and the table happens to be missing or someone has moved it to another corner of the room, it would come immediately to your attention.

This is how writers should perceive themselves during an immersion experience. Be present on a regular basis and stand back from a situation so you are not in the way and you do not pose a threat. If you have questions, do not interrupt the action taking place to ask them; I always save my questions for a time when the person I am shadowing seems to be in a reflective mood.

Although I will sometimes spend hours with subjects without directly communicating with them, and I will come and go without greetings or goodbyes, I am always amazed and delighted to discover that, like the missing living room table, they always notice when I suddenly disappear for a few days. When I return to observe, they are usually anxious to brief me about all of the action I missed.

One of the best compliments I have ever been paid came from the legendary liver transplant pioneer Thomas Starzl, whose egocentric personality I was able to capture in a rare and intimate way. When asked by a journalist how it was that I could have pierced his usually resistant armor, Starzl replied: "I tell you, I never saw the guy." This means that I was never in his face. I followed Starzl and his entourage of assistants relentlessly, always remaining a few feet behind them, writing everything down as I walked.

10.5 Opening the "Access" Door

To this point, the discussion has focused on how to act (and how to gain additional access) once the door has been opened and certain privileges have been granted to a writer. But how to open the door is often a more formidable challenge.

Obviously, an experienced writer has the great advantage; showing your good, published work in essays and articles sends visions of understanding and national recognition dancing in the heads of your potential subjects. The more published work you can show, the easier it is to prove yourself.

Whether or not we have samples and clippings, we all possess certain strengths, ways to appeal to people with whom we want to spend time. Ask the obvious questions about yourself in an effort to find ways in which you and the person or people in whom you have interest might connect.

Do you have mutual friends (perhaps you live in the same neighborhood) or mutual interests (perhaps you both own motorcycles)? If you are a college student, perhaps some of the people you want to spend time with have children of their own in college: The poor-struggling-student appeal often is successful.

I always try to avoid the public relations departments of organizations I want to write about, at least until I reach the people in whom I have direct interest. Notice that I say "try." Public-relations types have a natural tendency to attempt to manage or control the information coming out of the organizations they represent. It's their job! Because they often have some sort of writing background, they more clearly understand (or have time to consider) the implications of a writer getting inside access.

How to work around a public relations department and contact a busy person who is shielded by secretaries and security guards? I have been very successful in writing letters to people at their homes, addresses that often can be found in the phone book or through the nationwide telephone directories available on CD-ROM. Faxing can also be effective. Many executives monitor their fax machines, whereas underlings or secretaries screen their mail. So too with e-mail, although it has been difficult to obtain e-mail addresses until now.

10.6 Going Through the Back Door

Previously, I advised that you should not work for the people you are writing about while you are writing. That does not mean that you cannot take a job in a bagel bakery or as a hospital orderly or on the grounds crew at Yankee Stadium in order to gain, at least on a temporary basis, a special insider's insight. This foot-in-the-door approach will usually lead an enterprising writer somewhere special.

There are also many public places that, over a period of time, could lead to good immersion stories without the advantage of special privileges. Because of the legal complications that may come into play, it would be rare for a judge in a criminal court, for example, to open the door to his chambers and allow a writer to hang out. But sitting in the same judge's courtroom over a period of time and watching him in action, getting to know the courtroom hangers-on, the law clerks, security guards and other regulars, listening to conversations, and observing the everyday drama of the courtroom experience often will lead to an interesting and graphic essay or book.

One of the classic profiles in creative nonfiction history, "Hub Fans Bid Kid Adieu," was written by the novelist John Updike about the legendary baseball star Ted Williams without the author ever interviewing the man Boston fans both admired and resented because of his athletic skill and personal egocentricity. Updike went to games at Fenway Park off and on and talked baseball with fans vociferously through the season, but he framed his essay around a nine-inning game at Fenway—Williams's last as a professional, the day before he retired. That game was also the scene of Williams's last professional home run.

The "Frank Sinatra Has a Cold" profile to which I have previously referred is perhaps better and certainly different because Sinatra is more vulnerable when revealed through the eyes of the many others interviewed by Gay Talese (remember, Sinatra with a cold had refused to talk with Talese), than he would have been if he had been speaking for himself.

10.7   How Long Do Immersions Take?

In most cases, immersions specifically and book projects generally are never actually completed when predicted or expected. The Pulitzer Prize-winning historian David McCullough once told me that he never actually started to write his books until he could not think of one more question to ask or fact to unearth. But by the time he finished the first draft of his book, months or years later, he realized that he was perhaps only half to two thirds done with the research.

I have had similar experiences, immersing myself in a subject or hanging around with a person until I could think of nothing more to ask or to learn. This is the signal that it is time to isolate yourself from the immersion and commit your experience to words. This first attempt to write will reveal the gaps in your research, which forces you to return to relive certain parts of the experience, sometimes repeatedly. I usually will go back and forth three or four times until my essay or book seems complete.

11

Interviewing

11.1 The Art of Listening

Writers must learn to be focused listeners and be willing to commit the time necessary to establish trust between themselves and their subjects. This is an especially valuable asset when the people about whom you are writing feel isolated and alone. Most of the surgeons I met had little desire to converse with their patients on a personal level. These doctors were busy, and distanced themselves both from patients whose lives were in jeopardy and from the patients' families.

Being a good listener in an atmosphere of isolation leads to many poignant situations in which excruciating and vivid moments of truth can be achieved. I will never forget my midnight conversation with a dying woman, Becky Little, who fought heroically to maintain her sanity after waking up from what she had assumed would be routine liver surgery, only to discover that she had received a liver transplant—a shock and a violation she could hardly endure.

There was no need to dramatize or describe the hospital room scene: The drama was inherent in Becky's thoughts and words, especially when it was discovered that the cancer that had necessitated the transplant had returned:

> It is hard to say now that I am not glad that I had the
> transplant because otherwise I would have been dead a year

ago. Yet so often I think I would have been better off dead, and that way it would be over with. Sometimes I think that all it's done is to prolong the misery. If I would have died because I didn't have a transplant, then I wouldn't have gone through all the pain I am going through now.

A similar situation occurs in a story I once wrote about a wealthy businesswoman, Pauline, who spent $50,000 in order to keep her beloved cat alive through diabetes, surgeries, and chemotherapy, to no avail. Her cat dies. Now, although she has her husband, Dick, she feels all alone without her doctors or her pet. She wants to talk, but no one is there to listen, except for me.

> Once we were in the kitchen having dinner when Baby Cat took a seizure. Dick, her husband, panicked. He said, "Do something. Save him." I got Gene [veterinarian Solomon] on the line and explained what was happening, "Just tell me what to do."
>
> He said, "Okay. Just take a deep breath. Now follow exactly. You've got to be my eyes right now, Pauline." And I did exactly what he said. . . . because the animal was almost dead. There was no movement. He was laying there with his mouth sort of open. Finally he began to come around. And then Gene said, "All right, I'll meet you at the hospital."
>
> This was midnight on a Sunday December night. We all piled into the car. My husband was crying. I never admitted it then because I had to be strong, but I was falling apart. I never thought we'd make it to Gene. But in situations like that, someone has to be strong and take charge.
>
> Like the time Baby Cat fell out of the window—the year before I met Gene. A real crisis situation. I thought I was going to die because, for one thing, this was my mistake. It was the middle of the winter. I was in the bathroom getting dressed to go to a meeting, and it

felt stuffy, so I had opened a window. I was putting on blusher, and suddenly I heard this horrible screeching sound. I walked to the window, looked out, and there's my cat. Down on the ground, four stories below, screaming. Well, I went crazy. I nearly fell out the window myself. . . .

I was wearing a top, a half-slip and high heels, but I didn't care. I ran downstairs and out to the parking lot. It was beginning to snow. That is probably what attracted him: the snowflakes. Baby Cat was a bloody mess. I scooped him up. I was screaming for help. Nobody came out. I really don't know how I got up in the elevators, but got to someone's door, and I'm kicking it. A man came to the door. I said, "Come with me immediately."

He said, "What's the matter?"

I said, "Don't ask questions, I need help. Come into my apartment. Fast." In the apartment, I said, "Get on the phone. Get the number of the Animal Medical Center."

He said, "Where is your telephone book?"

I'll never forget that stupid question. I was livid. You know what I did? I kicked him in the shins! I said, "Call Information—now. Do you hear me?"

And all this time, I'm holding onto the cat, who is thrashing and screaming. So he got the number and he makes the call. He got the address. He said, "The Animal Medical Center said to put him on a board."

I said, "I haven't got a board. What else did they say?"

"They said wrap him in something warm."

Now, two other neighbors who saw what happened, Mickey and Roberta, came in. I ran to my closet and grabbed my mink coat and wrapped Baby Cat up in it. Roberta tried to take it away. "You'll get it all bloody; it'll be ruined."

I said, "Get your hands off of it. Get down to the car."

Mickey is a driver who usually putzes along at 20 miles

an hour. But she went down that boulevard at 90. She went through red lights. I said, "Drive faster."

We get to the hospital. They put me on an elevator with Baby Cat. They are about to take him away when the doctor sees that I am hysterical and stops and says, "Come with me for just a second."

I don't know where the hell he ever took me, but there was some long corridor that finally ended up in this little tiny room with no window, three walls and a door. Tiny. And I'm saying, "Why are you taking me back here right now? You should be up there helping my animal. Why are you doing this?"

And he says to me, "Scream."

I said, "I have no time to scream. Don't worry about me. Take care of my animal. Just do what you're supposed to do."

"I said scream."

"I don't feel like screaming. Get help for the cat."

Do you know what he did? He pinched me! I was black and blue for a week. He grabbed me and twisted me so hard, I burst into tears. I stood there and I cried. I cried torrents for two or three minutes. And then he said, "Are you okay now?"

I said, "Yeah."

He said, "Okay, let's go see the animal."

11.2   Speaking in "Scenes"

Throughout this book, I have stressed the importance of telling a story through a series of scenes. It is essential to understand that although a writer may be doing something as traditional as interviewing, the results of good interviewing are also story-oriented, as in the above monologue. As an interviewer, I ask questions that lead to long and detailed answers that are turned into stories.

In fact, I never ask a subject about whom I am writing for an interview, which connotes an official question-answer hierarchy. I always say that I have a number of subjects about his or her life and/or profession that I want to discuss. "Is there a time in the near future when we can sit down and talk?"

On meeting someone for the first time, I might request a get-acquainted interview, which is purposefully official, designed to establish a relationship between writer and subject and to discuss the guidelines around which we might work together in an immersion experience. I might also request an informational interview from an expert in a particular field. But if I want to get to know someone and expect to invest a long period of time shadowing him or her, I will try to avoid language that structures or limits my approach.

11.3 Interviewing Paraphernalia

I have referred to the use of my notebook. I try to show it periodically during an immersion just to remind people about what I am doing. I think this is only fair, although earlier in my career I practiced Gay Talese's technique of going to great lengths to conceal the tools of the journalistic trade in order not to call attention to myself as a writer or minimize the spontaneity of the situation.

Talese does carry a notebook, but he tries to keep as many of the details of a situation as possible in his head until he can slip into a men's room or some other private place to write down what he has overheard and attempted to remember.

Talese also does not believe in tape recorders. After his immersion is over for the day, he will try to get to a typewriter or computer as quickly as possible and write down everything he can remember about the experience he observed that day. He believes that tape recorders make writers lazy.

In his own case, being interviewed by writers with tape recorders ("I see them half-listening, nodding pleasantly and relaxing in the knowledge that the little wheels are rolling") is a waste of time. "What they are getting from me is not the insight that comes from deep probing and perceptive analysis and old-fashioned legwork; it is rather the first draft of my mind. . . ."

New Yorker staff writer Alec Wilkinson recently told me that he usually does not take notes during experiences he witnesses or interviews he conducts; he has to concentrate on the conversation with his subject so that his follow-up questions are sensitive and intelligent and he can maintain eye contact with the interviewee. After interviews, Wilkinson will jump in his car, drive around the corner and out of sight, and immediately commit everything he can remember to words on a yellow legal tablet.

11.4   The Bumbling Approach to Reporting

Lest you think I am condoning the spontaneous, undocumented approach to the art of interviewing, as practiced by the aforementioned writers and many others, here is William L. Howarth's description of the masterful John McPhee while interviewing, from *The John McPhee Reader*, a "must read" for any creative nonfiction writer.

> When McPhee conducts an interview, he tries to be as blank as his notebook pages, totally devoid of preconceptions, equipped with only the most elementary knowledge . . . at times his speech slows, his brow knits, he asks the same question over and over. When repeating answers, he so garbles them that a new answer must be provided. Some informants find his manner relaxing, others are exasperated; in either case, they talk more freely and fully to him than they normally would to a reporter. While McPhee insists that his air of density is not a deliberate ruse, he does not deny its useful results. Informants may be timid or hostile unless they feel superior or equal to their interviewer. By repeating and even fumbling their answers, McPhee encourages people to embroider a topic until he has its entirety. In an ideal interview, he listens without interrupting, at liberty to take notes without framing repartee or otherwise entering the conversation.

11.5   Fact Checking

Most magazines will carefully fact check articles and essays they publish. I have worked with fact checkers from *The New Yorker*, *The Atlantic Monthly*, and *The New York Times Magazine* on articles and essays I have written for them and I have come to see that fact checkers are relentless. Although the work is painstaking and often boring, especially when you are forced to look through a pile of information that you gathered as much as a year or more ago to isolate the source of a fact, detail, or quotation, it is also essential. I have always been appreciative of the fact checking experience because, invariably, the substance and the credibility of my story is improved. Attorneys representing book publishers will diligently examine book manuscripts prior to publication for instances of potential litigation—libel, slander. Unfortunately, in book publishing, however, responsibility for fact checking rests solely on the author's shoulders.

This is the text for a photo-feature that I recently sold to *The New York Times Magazine* as I wrote it before fact checking and editing.

"A Horse of a Different Color"

Last year, when veterinarians at New Bolton Center, the rural campus of the University of Pennsylvania's School of Veterinary Medicine, were asked to examine a horse named Cam Fella, who had developed a malignant testicular tumor, they were perplexed—and perhaps a little intimidated. Cam Fella, the most distinguished pacer in the history of harness racing, is not an ordinary former champion: He is the most valuable breeding stallion in the world. Since retiring in 1984, the 16-year-old's progeny have amassed the highest average earnings of any stud—standardbred or thoroughbred. Cam Fella's stud fees generate nearly $3 million annually.

Normally, a horse with testicular cancer would be castrated to prevent metastases; the remaining testicle could manufacture sperm. Cam Fella, however, was a "ridgling"; he had only one descended testicle. Castration would save his life, but end his career, unless veterinarians could find a way to eliminate the tumor. Their solution, after weeks of consultation, was freezing the tumor away. Cryotherapy had been used in horses before, but Dr. William J. Donawick, Professor of Surgery, arranged for the use of a newly developed instrument called AccuProbe, which delivers precise amounts of liquid nitrogen with pinpoint accuracy.

Solving the puzzle of a testicular tumor isn't the only reason Cam Fella's owners approached Donawick. New Bolton facilities are specially designed to expedite a half-ton horse through surgery and recuperation without damage—a major apprehension in the equine world ever since the champion thoroughbred, Ruffian, broke its leg in a nationally televised race two decades ago and, after undergoing surgical repair, broke its leg a second time in an anesthesia recovery stall.

A unique feature at New Bolton is a recovery pool where horses can awaken from anesthesia and thrash without hurting themselves or anyone else. Cam Fella's pool recoveries after four cryosurgeries have been flawless. "He's not lame or sore," says Donawick. "He walks and runs the day after surgery." Anesthesiologist Kim Olson, who interacts with Cam Fella most frequently, observes that "surgery seems to bore him."

Although cryotherapy and ultrasound equipment were donated, New Bolton charged its standard rate for services, facilities, and a dozen nurses and doctors: $2,989.71. "We researched what the entire procedure might cost if this had been done on a person," said Bob Tucker, owner of Stonegate Farms in New Jersey, where Cam Fella lives: "It was at least $50,000."

In between tumor-reducing treatments, Cam Fella was bred more than 100 times during the February through July breeding season, resulting in 62 mares in foal at last count.

At least one additional cryosurgery will follow. Donawick hopes to eradicate the tumor before the end of the year.

Here is the same story *after fact checking and editing.* Notice some of the mistakes I made that the fact checker was able to isolate and change, including Cam Fella's annual fees, and the surgeon who was responsible for this revolutionary operation. It is important to note that my research was not particularly flawed—I could document the information that I provided. But in confirming my work, the fact checker probed more deeply. In the process, she discovered that Donawick was actually following the lead of Dr. Kenney, whose work was interrupted by a partially debilitating illness. And when she confronted the owners with the $3 million earnings figure, they amended the final number on their own. Notice also the change in quotation from "person" to "going rate," in order to make the experience more accurate.

"Cam Fella Goes Under the Knife"*

Cam Fella, one of the most distinguished pacers in the history of harness racing, is no ordinary former champion; he is the most valuable standardbred breeding stallion in the world. Since his retirement in 1984, 10 of his progeny have earned $1 million or more apiece. Cam Fella's stud fees generate at least $2.5 million annually.

So when veterinarians discovered last year that Cam Fella had testicular cancer, his owners were alarmed. Normally, the diseased testicle would be removed and the remaining testicle left to continue manufacturing sperm. Cam Fella, however, was a "ridgling": he had only one viable testicle. Castration would save his life, but end his reproductive career.

Veterinarians at the New Bolton Center in Philadelphia,

*First published in *The New York Times Magazine* August 27, 1995. Copyright © 1995 by The New York Times. Reprinted by permission.

part of the University of Pennsylvania's School of Veterinary Medicine, proposed a radical solution: freeze and destroy the tumor with a series of treatments. Horses had been treated with cryotherapy before, but Dr. Robert Kenney, a reproduction specialist, arranged for the use of a newly developed instrument—previously used only on human patients—called Accuprobe, which delivers precise amounts of liquid nitrogen with pinpoint accuracy.

The New Bolton Center is the world's premier equine hospital, designed to see a half-ton horse safely through surgery and recovery. Because the cryotherapy and ultrasound equipment were lent by its developers, the hospital charged Cam Fella only for its facilities and staff: $2,989.71. "We researched what the procedure might cost if this had been done at the going rate," said Bob Tucker, owner of Stonegate Standardbred Farms in New Jersey, where Cam Fella lives. "It was at least $50,000."

The Elusive Truth

12.1 Permission to Lie?

During a talk to one of my graduate level (MFA) classes at the University of Pittsburgh, Jane Bernstein, author of the memoir *Loving Rachel*, a book about a family's ability to come to grips with the birth of a severely handicapped child and the inevitable adjustments and accommodations that follow, made a statement that ignited controversy and fueled a debate that lasted the entire term.

Bernstein, who had previously published two novels, was discussing the difficulty of making a transition from fiction to nonfiction—learning to apply all the techniques and devices she had utilized in fiction to her nonfiction—without altering the truth.

When she began writing this book about her family she found herself blocked by habit and by the conflict between the two genres. "I couldn't write—or rather, I couldn't write the way I wanted to write. And so," said Bernstein, "I had no choice. In order to get my book going, I had to grant myself *permission to lie*." To put it another way, she approached her book project with the three-dimensional frame of mind of the novelist.

Bernstein did not mean that she wanted to make up facts or tell stories that were not true. But the narrow range of creative options traditionally granted to a journalist inhibited her writing. Giving herself "permission to lie" permitted expansive thinking; it allowed three-dimensional thought and scenic expression in a novelistic context. In other words, she did not allow her writing momentum to be interrupted by the literal truth of what happened to her daughter Rachel and the rest of the family. She recreated ideas and details from memory, as best as she could.

After her first draft was completed from beginning to end and the revision and rewriting process was launched, Bernstein removed or repaired the "lies" she had inserted. From her point of view, *Loving Rachel* was as true and honest as possible. She then submitted complete drafts of the book to her husband and to the half-dozen physicians who had worked with or counseled her family over the years. They returned the manuscripts without so much as a single change. Giving herself permission to lie led to as true a document as possible—from all of the players' points of view.

It is important to point out that Bernstein was working from memory; she had taken few notes about the first year of Rachel's life, on which the book was centered. Rachel's long-range health and her entire family's future was in jeopardy. Bernstein did not have the time to write down everything that had happened to her while she was living it.

It is not certain that the physicians who fact checked her manuscript actually said, verbatim, exactly what Bernstein remembered that they said, and whether the conversations and the scenes and the surroundings were exactly as Bernstein had reported them. But according to the characters involved in the experience—the people about whom she was writing—her version or reconstruction was conceivable—a correct approximation. "It sounds right and it reads right," one of the physicians had said.

But whether it was exactly, literally, word-for-word true, the reader will never know. Bernstein will never know, either, I suspect. It probably was not. But clearly, granting herself permission to lie probably had not significantly altered the factual reality of the book—or else the physicians, who were not all presented as positive figures, would have objected.

12.2   The Literal Accuracy of Quotations

Sending a draft of an essay or article to people about whom you have written and asking them to review it for factual discrepancies is a touchy situation.

Many writers feel that they have gotten their subjects to make certain admissions and to provide delicate information, and that when subjects come face to face with their own words and feelings they might want to take it all back. This is a chance you take allowing subjects to review your work, and I do not always do it. But in situations in which you trust your information, it is always the most expedient method of self-protection.

Not that the people about whom you write, especially when you are working with them over a period of many months, will remember exactly what they have told you in interviews and conversations. In fact, people have often told me that they do not remember details about a conversation about which I have written or of making a specific statement, but in the same breath they will also often say, "But I could have—or I would have. It reflects what I truly believe."

Fact checking with Eric Parente ("The Quitter") turned out to be a terrific experience for me and an opportunity to improve my book. Although I had spent a significant amount of time with him, I only learned about his own personal adventures in the thoroughbred racing world *after* I allowed him to read "The Quitter" and amend some of the information I had written. The information about the psychology of approaching and dealing with horses also came after the fact checking. Or, to put it another way, after he learned to trust me.

But a writer never really knows what aspects of conversations, ideas, or incidents will touch a nerve with a subject. I am often amazed at what people actually complain about. I was once telephoned by a heart transplant surgeon whom I had quoted extensively in *Many Sleepless Nights*. I was momentarily wary when he identified himself on the telephone, and when I heard the serious tone of his voice.

I had given him sections of my book in which he appeared to review. As it turned out, of the many pages of quoted conversations, he objected to only one word—a vulgarity he used quite frequently. As a favor, he asked if I would delete that word, or substitute a more benign alternative for it, because his mother would read the book and he did not want her to know how much he swore. Of course, I complied.

12.3 Doctoring Quotations

A liberty or license that creative nonfiction writers might take is to doctor or clean up quotations to make them more readable or understandable or to fit more smoothly into a longer narrative. A few journalists insist that they have never changed a quotation, and there is no reason not to believe them. But they are part of a very small minority. There are numerous legitimate reasons to make such changes or alterations. People being interviewed often are not as articulate or as careful as they might want to be. Usually, when you make such a change, you reconfirm the quotation or conversation with the parties involved.

The concept and conflicts of truth and literary license require continuous clarification and careful analysis. The idea of granting "permission to lie" or fabricate for the sake of clarity is dangerous. Notice in some examples in this book characters actually reveal what they are thinking. But notice, too, that I do not quote or literally recreate actual thought, a common over indulgence of creative nonfiction writers.

Writers who actually "quote" thoughts take the chance of losing credibility, because readers know that writers cannot hear their subjects think. An obvious and frequently employed technique that allows a writer to report thought literally is taking a direct approach: Ask the people about whom you are writing what they are thinking at any given time. If the tell you, then you possess a special license to recreate thought.

There exists a major difference between recreation and fabrication, however, and there are a number of literary licenses that potentially could lead to litigation, with writers at the short end of the stick.

12.4 Compression

A case involving *New Yorker* writer Janet Malcolm and psychoanalyst Jeffrey Masson was recently resolved in the courts after ten long and expensive years of litigation. It began with a technique or device many creative nonfiction writers use called "compression." This is the common practice of gathering bits and pieces of conversations—large chunks of quotation—and moving them around, squishing or compressing them into one long conversation. Masson accused Malcolm not only of compressing information but of literally making up quotations.

Some traditional journalists find compression highly unethical and objectionable, but most creative nonfiction writers will admittedly compress—combine quotes, conversations, incidents, and so on—in order to control material more easily, allowing the writer to craft a more readable essay or article.

In the scene in a previous chapter showing veterinarian Wendy Freeman dis-budding a calf, for example, let us say that I actually observed Freeman dis-budding five calves, gathered my details and quotations, and compressed them into one incident. This did not happen, incidentally, but it could have happened, and I might very well have compressed for the sake of dramatic impact and efficiency, provided *that I did not misconstrue the inherent truth of the experience, misquote Freeman, or mislead my readers about Freeman.* I do not oppose compression, but writers must be wary of the consequences.

Once again, if a writer compresses information, then fact checking with the people involved in the experience is vital.

For memoirs, many writers will recreate scenes or conversations that took place long ago, and sometimes fact checking with others is not possible.

But usually these memories are as much a part of the writer's life as anyone else's, thereby allowing a much larger window for literary license and general speculation. Here's what the prolific novelist and essayist Paul West told interviewer Barbara Adams about truth and accuracy in nonfiction.

"I like writing nonfiction, but I really get off writing fiction. It's more libidinous," he chuckles. But surely there are satisfactions unique to nonfiction, I venture. He has the impish answer ready: "You can irritate your family more. The fiction doesn't irritate anybody because they don't take it seriously, I guess. But nonfiction they go through with a fine-toothed comb, saying 'No, you got that wrong, and that! Why don't you give this up, because clearly you don't have the talent for it.' " He laughs, perversely gratified.

Writing memoirs, I say, is a double bind: Your subjects expect accuracy or literalism and at the same time may resent appropriation of any part of their lives. West nods, "Oh god, yes. They expect you to be them, to report events as if you were them, and then they completely ignore the fact that a) you're a novelist and b) you're a stylist, and this takes you very far from predictable lines of reportage. This doesn't bother me and never will. Because ultimately this is the big issue that I make of words, and that's more important than the basic facts. Writing is always a stylistic opportunity, and I'm sure that doesn't appeal to family members."

West finds the novel "always more open to manipulation," whereas nonfiction is more deliberate. "You are, I suppose, restricted to certain facts—you know, the way your father walked. You're not going to mess with that too much." But West admits to "messing with" his own thoughts and actions a great deal, and even inventing characters in nonfiction—"just to see what'll happen." In "My Mother's Music," he introduces a fictional character, the allusively named Reyner Rilka, providing his mother, in her nineties, with an additional friend and neighbor. Always tinkering, the novelist argues for invention: "The grouping wasn't right; I needed a male wall to bounce things off."

Despite his restructuring of reality, West believes his mother would certainly have recognized herself in this memoir, in which he sought to make her "dominant on every page." Writing about his father, however, as West did in "I, Said the Sparrow" (1963), an autobiography up to age 17, was unappreciated. "He hated it—he said it exposed and revealed him. He hated to be depicted or even mentioned. And of course he shows up a lot in the recent novel *Love's Mansion*—with a sex life he never had, I'm sure. He would have been aggrieved, I think. So you can't really get away with it." He pauses, then hastens to a more positive thought: "My mother liked it; she liked being written about. She'd nod and say 'You've got a very accurate eye' or something. I say very little about my sister because she doesn't care to be written about either. If I'm writing about her, I know I'm getting it wrong, ipso facto, so I cut it to the minimum."[1]

12.5 Who Knows the Real Truth?

As indicated in an earlier chapter, the truth is often larger than any single fact, not a cut-and-dried positive or negative value. It is quite elusive and, like beauty, in the eye of the beholder.

It turns out that what I saw in the heart-transplant world resonated with the surgeon with whom I worked. This does not mean that we concur with every single fact and detail along the way. So, too, with Jane Bernstein's *Loving Rachel*. The physicians intimately involved agreed that it sounded right. Bernstein thought that it was right, too, but she could not and would not vouch for the absolute essence of truth.

But if you stand back from the situation and think about it, this makes sense. Think about your own experience with your parents, spouses, or employer. Haven't you been involved in countless conversations in which two or more people experience or recall the same conversation quite differently? Imagine putting a video camera on the shoulders of each participant in a dispute, a game, or a debate. Even though the experience and the location is shared, because of each participant's angles and nuances, each interpretation will be skewed.

All of this is especially true and relevant in a memoir. Margaret Gibson's recollection of the killing of the rabbit and Don Morrill's memory of his neighborhood may not reflect the recollections of their parents or other participants. Edward's attitude toward Margaret, Betsy,

---

[1]From Barbara Adams, "The Essayist at Work," *Creative Nonfiction* 6, pp 21–34.

or Aunt T, and his job of beheading chickens might significantly clash with the quiet and romantic way he is presented. Think about how Mrs. Whittenhall perceived the kids of the neighborhood—probably a completely different way than the way they perceived her or they thought she perceived them.

Previously, I discussed researching and interviewing techniques, pointing out that Gay Talese and Alec Wilkinson abhorred tape recorders. Talese jotted down a few notes, then waited to recreate the interview or experience until he returned home, hours or days later. Wilkinson jumped in a car, drove around the corner and parked in order to get down the words and ideas as soon as possible. Surely this work cannot be completely accurate, although the essence and the intention are clearly correct. Otherwise, they might be facing litigation.

Which brings us back once again to Janet Malcolm, Jeffrey Masson, and litigation. Masson was not talking about doctoring or cleaning up quotations when he sued Malcolm; he was accusing Malcolm, an experienced and established *New Yorker* contributor, of outright fabrication.

There were actually five disputed parts of the 45,000-word essay, published in 1983, with which Masson went to court. In the first trial, a jury actually found that all five passages that Masson questioned were, indeed, fabricated and that two were libelous. But when the jury deadlocked over the amount of damages to be awarded, a judge ruled that the entire case was to be retried. The second jury reversed the first, ruling that only two of the five quotations were fabricated, but that neither were libelous.

On the surface this may still seem to be a victory for Masson, but it was not, because the jury also concluded that neither quotation demonstrated that Malcolm acted with the recklessness required to be deemed libel and thereby be assessed damages.

12.6 Who Is the Final Arbiter?

Although Malcolm and Masson were equal participants in the experience, it was Masson's—not Malcolm's—life that was being exposed, and his reputation (at least prior to the lawsuit) that was being questioned.

In writing more personally, as in a memoir, it is your life that is being unmasked, as well as the lives of the other members of your family. You have a perfect right to tell your story in your way, and it is very unlikely that a family member will take you to court and even less likely that the litigation will go very far.

You may be reluctant to be completely truthful about the people in your immediate family, for whom you may care a great deal, for fear of hurting or humiliating them. But this is a personal problem you are confronting, chances are, not a legal one. For more information and enlightenment about such problems, I recommend Jonathan Kirsch's *Handbook of Publishing Law* (Venice, CA: Acrobat Books, 1995).

13

In Conclusion

13.1 Following the Frame

My students constantly worry about the ending of books, essays, or articles, a problem that receives much more attention than it deserves. Not that endings are not important, but they will also be one of the easier problems to solve—if the essay or book possesses the structural and creative integrity we have been discussing from the beginning.

If, as you near the end of the book or essay, you suddenly find that you are lost, unable to move your narrative in any direction, then I would direct you back to the beginning and remind you to follow your overall story structure or frame.

Remember that in addition to compelling a reader to enter into your essay, a lead scene should reflect a focus and a story or plot that will be carried through, at least subtly, from beginning to end. If this is not the case—if you are unable to follow a trail, albeit vague and ragged, of scenes and stories, back and forth, beginning to end, then perhaps your structure is flawed.

In other words, at some point during the development of a book or essay, writers should know where they are going. During the writing process, they may decide that they do not want to go in the direction they are headed, and they may change directions a dozen times. But the conclusion should come as part of the ebb and flow of the narrative.

A lack of direction in the end telegraphs a lack of direction in the beginning and middle as well.

I did not know when I started writing "The Incident" for *Stuck in Time* exactly how I would end my book, 300 pages later, but I knew that there would be a logical connection, a way of linking with the story and theme I had planted in the very beginning.

Indeed, Jeanne Marie Laskas begins "The Garden in Winter" with the dual themes of a train ride and gardening. She ends 3,000 words later in a similar manner, with her hands in the dirt on a free-fall journey right through China. Margaret Gibson and Donald Morrill have written essays that reflect multiple themes from beginning to end. Refer to the Readings section to see how *Stuck in Time* concludes.

13.2 Abolish Title-Mania

Although the title represents the reader's first connection to a book or essay, it ought to be the writer's last consideration, if it is a consideration at all. A good title is not important, but remember that it reflects the focus or the essence of your project. Whatever title you choose in the beginning, it will change as many times as you change your own mind about what you are doing and where you are going.

Editors will also have their own ideas about the essence and quality of titles they want to appear in the pages of their magazines and journals. Often, titles will be written in certain ways to appeal to readers or book buyers.

In fact, book titles are often determined by the sales manager of the publishing company, rather than by the author or editor. This makes sense from a profit-and-loss point of view. If the sales or marketing staff maintains that they cannot sell a book to store owners because of a title or if the marketing representative insists that a book will be displayed in the wrong section of a book store or catalogued inappropriately at the library, then the title must be changed.

Such was the case with Jeanne Marie Laskas' first collection of essays, *The Balloon Lady and Other People I Know*, which was originally titled for its lead essay (which was, coincidentally, "The Garden in Winter").

But the conventional marketing wisdom was that Laskas' book would be typecast as a gardening or horticultural work, which is far from true.

As you can see, the title of my transplant book changed from "The Replaceable Body" to "Many Sleepless Nights" in the course of the book's development. My favorite title for my own work was actually dreamed up by a sales manager, after my editor and I were stumped for weeks: *The Best Seat in Baseball, But You Have to Stand!: The Game as Umpires See It.*

13.3 Be Happy Your Reader Survived to the End

This is another reason why I do not worry too much about endings. If my writing and my ideas have been strong enough to compel my reader to cruise through my book or essay from beginning to end, and I have said pretty much everything I think is important in the pages in between, then I have achieved my objectives. At that point I will assume that I have fulfilled my contract with my reader, and I will find a gracious way to say goodbye. In the case of this book, I am not going to say goodbye, however. Instead, I will offer you my e-mail address (lgu+@pitt.edu) just in case you have any questions or comments.

Appendix 1

A Sample Book Proposal

Publishers realize that works of nonfiction require a great deal of time, effort, and expense. So, more often than not, writers may receive a contract for a book, plus a cash advance (against future royalties) based on a well-rendered proposal. As a model for your own efforts, here is the book proposal accepted by W.W. Norton for *Many Sleepless Nights*.

Notice that it is written in a cinematic way, suggesting specific scenes, characters, and potential story lines or frames. My focus—what I think I would eventually teach my readers—is also included. I also outline my own qualifications. It is important to point out that editors do not necessarily expect that you will follow the proposals you write; editors understand that once you are involved in the experience, you might change your mind, go off on a dozen tangents, and gather new and important information that may completely alter the thesis of your initial proposal. This is part of the creative process.

But a detailed and well-planned proposal is required as proof that you understand how to structure and write a book, that the idea of framing, writing in scenes with dialogue and description, focusing, and so forth is within a particular writer's grasp. This proposal took three months to research and write, but it yielded immediate results.

"The Replaceable Body"

Although references to human organ transplants have been discovered in ancient Egyptian manuscripts, it wasn't until 1905 that Austrian ophthamologist Eduard Zirm lifted sections from the cornea of a dying 11-year-old boy and restored the sight of a workman blinded by lime. Nearly half a century later, doctors at Boston's Peter Bent Brigham Memorial Hospital successfully transplanted a kidney into Richard Herrick, who had been wasting away for more than a year. Another decade passed before Dr. Georges Mathe of the Gustave Roussy Institute near Paris saved the life of a man dying of leukemia with a total bone marrow transplant—the first in history. During that same year, 1963, the first human lung transplant was attempted at the University of Mississippi, and the first successful liver transplant was completed by Dr. Thomas E. Starzl of the Colorado Medical Center. Perhaps the most important and widely discussed transplant surgery of all time occurred in 1967, when South African Christiaan Barnard replaced the diseased heart of Louis Washkansky, a 55-year-old grocer who, upon awakening from the anesthetic after the operation, called himself "the new Frankenstein."

Louis Washkansky died from pneumonia just 18 days later, and during the next dozen years, many hundreds of transplant recipients died, primarily because of the body's natural tendency to reject foreign matter. But with the drug Cyclosporine, introduced in 1980 by Dr. Starzl, now at the University of Pittsburgh and Presbyterian-University Hospital, the world's major transplant center, and Dr. Norman E. Shumway of Stanford University Medical Center, one-year survival rates for heart transplants have reached 80 percent; for kidneys almost 90 percent. During the past three years at Presbyterian-University, surgeons have transplanted nearly 300 livers, 500 kidneys, 100 hearts, 10 heart-lungs and 30 pancreases. On Valentine's Day, 1984, Dr. Starzl saved the life of six-year-old Stormie Jones of Cumby, Texas, with a simultaneous heart-liver transplant—the first in the world.

A revolution in medicine and in surgery has taken place since Louis Washkansky opened his eyes and blinked in amazement, and it is the story behind this revolution, all of the hope and joy it has fostered, all of the problems it has caused, the disappointments it has created, which I plan to document in the book proposed on these pages.

Presby

More transplants are done here than anywhere else in the world: more livers, heart-lungs, kidneys, heart-livers, as well as bone marrow and pancreas transplants. Most of the research and testing of the drug Cyclosporine, which has made successful transplantation possible, was done at Presby. Surgeons from countries all over the world are trained in transplantation techniques first in the classroom at the University of Pittsburgh Medical School, and then, clinically, at Presby. What makes Presby unique is that it is an inner-city hospital, bordered by the ghetto, in an area burdened by one of the highest unemployment rates in the nation. And yet, it has always been at the forefront of medical science: Jonas Salk developed the vaccine for polio here and at Pitt nearly four decades ago.

Clearances

I have been granted access to all situations, people, and events related to transplantation at Presby. I am free to interview, and observe in action on a day-to-day basis, surgeons, social workers, nurses and other members of surgical and support teams, organ procurement specialists, as well as organ recipients and their families. I am permitted to observe surgery, sit in on patient–doctor conferences, attend the Tuesday staff meetings (where patients with priority for available organs are determined). I plan to be in the admitting room with social-service personnel when patients first come into contact with Presby's transplant team, and to follow many patients and their families through each step of the experience for as long as it might take. I will move into Family House, the reconditioned old Victorian home that serves as living quarters and support center for families of transplant patients, attend meetings, and come to know the members of TRIO (Transplant Recipients International Organization). I will also visit and investigate other transplant centers, including the Mayo Clinic in Rochester, Minnesota, which, with the help of Presby, is now organizing its own liver transplant unit.

Treatment/Structure

Transplant recipients pass through six stages of psychological adjustment, according to the Department of Psychiatry and Surgery, Arizona State University: (1) Evaluation Period; (2) Waiting Period; (3) Immediate Postsurgical Period; (4) Rejection Episode; (5) Recovery Period; (6) Discharge.

For *The Replaceable Body*, this is the order in which the vast and complicated story of transplantation will be told.

Point of View

I will focus upon the varied experiences of three or four patients who have lived, suffered, rejoiced, and perhaps even died while struggling through the six stages of adjustment. As the stories of these patients begin to unfold, the people (nurses, social workers, surgeons, procurement specialists, etc.) involved in the transplantation process will be introduced, the many physical and scientific complications stemming from transplantation will be presented, the ethical, practical, and moral issues surrounding transplantation will be discussed and debated. When possible, the experiences of the patients on whom I focus will be integrated from chapter to chapter, so that a panoramic picture of the world of organ transplantation, as depicted in this hospital and at this time in history, will eventually begin to surface.

Narrative Sequence

Based upon the patients and staff with whom I have come in contact and the information I have gathered so far—factors that may well change as I become more involved in the project—here is a tentative breakdown of the content and shape of the book.

I.   Evaluation

Last Resort

Eight-year-old Kimberly Fuller of Elk City, Oklahoma, arrived at Presbyterian-University Hospital on June 3, 1984 for evaluation as a possible heart-lung recipient. Although this was only the beginning of a process that might take years to complete, Kimberly's parents, David and Sandra, who accompanied her to Presby, had dedicated every spare moment during the past year to secure for their daughter this invaluable opportunity. Kimberly suffered from primary pulmonary hypertension, a fatal disease of the heart and lungs, which has no known treatment.

The Mayo Clinic had initially suggested the possibility of a transplant and referred the Fullers to the Stanford University Medical Center. Stanford had recommended Presby, where surgeons, much more practiced in multiple transplantation techniques, agreed to see Kimberly. But then David Fuller's health insurance carrier refused to provide the necessary advance deposit of $10,000 required by Presby for transplant evaluation. Facing the specter of months of additional delay, the Fullers arranged for a $10,000 second mortgage against the equity of their house, and finally, brought their child to Pittsburgh.

To date, the youngest person to have received a heart-lung transplant had been 19, but the little girl had one frightening factor in her favor: Without a transplant, Kimberly would die.

"For most people accepted into the transplantation program," said Donna Rinaldo, one of the three full-time social workers assigned to transplantation units at Presby, "transplantation is the last resort."

Your Money for Your Life

A social worker's initial objective is to determine whether the patient's insurance will cover the cost of the transplant. Currently, neither state

135

insurance agencies nor private health insurance carriers pay for transplantation surgery and the care and medicine it requires. Neither will Medicare pay the costs of transplantation, nor will Social Security in most cases. Hospitals have lost a great deal of money ($2.5 million at Presby since 1982) because of the confusion surrounding transplantation (whether it is considered experimental or routine surgery, and whether it is a necessity), and such confusion has led to the enforcement of strict new rules regarding the acceptance of potential transplant recipients.

If a patient does not qualify for coverage, a cash deposit of anywhere from $25,000 (kidney) to $200,000 (liver) is required. Recently, the governor of Pennsylvania, tired and frustrated after being asked repeatedly to make life and death decisions for every special plea, pressured the state insurance agency to accept transplantation claims. A few other states, including New York and Massachusetts, have followed Pennsylvania's lead, but most of the "Blues" and the private carriers continue to oppose it.

Media Magic

Soon after Kimberly Fuller arrived in Pittsburgh, Presby was visited by Oklahoma Governor George Nigh, along with a Tulsa newspaper reporter and a television crew. Governor Nigh had stopped to chat with one of his constituents, a 22-year-old mother of three, Terri Lenz, from Laverne, not far from Tulsa, who, coincidentally, also suffered from primary pulmonary hypertension, and had just recently received a heart-lung transplant. When the Oklahoma insurance commissioner had refused to guarantee the cost of her operation and treatment, a Tulsa TV station had launched a public service campaign on Terri's behalf, raising more than $300,000. Over the past few years, such media-made campaigns have become nearly commonplace around the country.

It didn't take long to arrange an on-camera meeting with Kimberly, her parents, and Governor Nigh. They sat in a lounge area attached to one of the transplant units, 10-3, Kimberly in a crisp new nightgown, a steel cylinder of oxygen at her side to help her breathe, and the Governor in his striped tie, ten-gallon hat, and neatly pressed pinstripe suit, together bent over a map of Oklahoma, spread out over a small table. Kimberly was extremely precocious and amazingly articulate, describing the state of her health and the complications of her disease in detail. Kimberly later revealed that her mother had trained her for weeks at home, with a "borrowed Mr. Microphone outfit," for the possibility of such an encounter.

Governor Nigh was asked only one question—the inevitable and embarrassing question. "What if surgeons at Presby agree to attempt Kimberly's operation? Will the Governor's office help guarantee the deposit to pay the bills?"

"I will do what we all do in time of trouble," said Nigh, a seasoned politician, "by joining the Fullers and all Oklahomans, and putting my trust and faith in God."

II.   Waiting Period

Tuesday Organ Meetings

Assuming that the financial problems can be resolved (more later), the Fullers will return home after the evaluation to wait in suspense and in limbo for the day on which they are finally summoned to the hospital for the operation. That day depends very much upon what happens each Tuesday at 10 A.M. at Presby.

There are separate meetings for liver, heart, kidney, and pancreas patients, each attended by Drs. Thomas E. Starzl and Chief of Surgery Henry Bahnson, as well as other surgeons on the staff, the Organ Procurement Coordinator, Donald E. Denny, and social workers assigned to transplant units. The objective is to discuss the organs that might be available and the condition of the patients in line for transplants. One by one, the attending physician will assess the health and well-being, status and location of each and every patient. When possible, the social worker will comment upon the emotional state of the patient and the family. How much longer can they wait? How well are they managing to adjust to the pressure and the uncertainty of waiting?

In addition to Kimberly Fuller, 36-year-old Jerry Blanford and 17-year-old Ray Blasingame are also discussed. Blasingame, of Taos, New Mexico, has been waiting in Pittsburgh for many weeks, while Blanford is sick and marooned in Winnetka, Illinois, in his son's one-bedroom second-floor apartment.

How Many Livers Will It Take?

There are obvious considerations governing the selection of the transplant recipient—size and weight of the available organ, blood type and age of the prospective patient. Within these parameters, transplant recipients are taken in chronological order. The overriding factor, however, is always need.

Ray Blasingame was passed over in the liver rotation four times in two months, first because the available liver was too large, second because the next liver was too small. The third liver "broke" while being transferred from the cooler in which it was carried. The fourth time, Ray was wheeled into the operating room—and then wheeled out again when Jerry Blanford suddenly arrived in Pittsburgh, bloated with fluid and blood, and with only hours to live. Blasingame finally got his liver on the fifth try. He and Blanford have since become best friends.

Blanford, by the way, gained much more than a new liver and a good friend through his transplantation ordeal. Before sickness made it impossible to work, he had managed a supermarket in a quiet blue-collar neighborhood, next door to a tavern where he and other local merchants often had lunch. The tavern was owned by a middle-aged woman with whom Blanford became friendly over the years. Because the tavern lacked a telephone, he often took messages on her behalf at the supermarket or called her from next door to the phone.

Blanford's illness had confused doctors at the Mayo Clinic, where he went initially for treatment. They knew that diabetes was at least one problem, but they needed a family medical history to provide a complete diagnosis. Blanford, however, was adopted. With his condition seriously deteriorating, Blanford's mother began searching for her son's natural parents.

Weeks later, a clerk answered the telephone at Blanford's supermarket and went to summon the woman who owned the tavern next door for a call. She smiled and waved at Jerry as she walked into the store and picked up the phone, but almost immediately her face turned ashen and her eyes went dim. She talked for a while, nodding and then saying a few quiet words, before hanging up and walking over to Jerry, who was sitting on a stool behind the cash register.

Then she told him that he was her son.

Although an organ was available when Blanford's need became critical, the process might not work so smoothly for Kimberly Fuller, no matter how ill she becomes. In her case, as in the case of Terri Lenz, two organs of the same size and weight from a donor with the same blood type must be available—simultaneously. Obviously, this makes the procurement problem doubly difficult. Terri had been on call, connected to Presby with a long-range beeper, for more than a year. Luckily, her condition had not seriously deteriorated during that time.

Unsung Hero

While Kimberly Fuller and her parents are waiting at home for a chance at renewed life, Donald Denny is sitting in his tiny office tucked into a far corner of the hospital, waiting for people to die.

Denny, a former high school teacher, along with 300 associates who work out of 110 organ transplant centers around the United States, have been called "the unsung heroes of organ transplantation" by surgeon Thomas Starzl. These men and women live their lives on a 24-hour treadmill; no moment is secure, no day is definite. Their schedule is determined by the unfortunate circumstances of strangers, often in another part of the country. The physical and moral pressure under which they constantly labor is severe.

At Presby over the past two years, 85 adults and children have died while awaiting liver transplants. About one-third of the candidates at Stanford die each year before a suitable heart is found. The problem is not a shortage of organs (Denny points out that there is a near surplus), but the process by which they are obtained.

Although polls show that the majority of Americans are favorably inclined toward donating organs, and 43 states make donor cards an integral part of the driver's license, the process becomes infinitely more complicated after the death occurs. Emergency medical crews and the hospital staff, engrossed in the lifesaving process, are much too busy and sometimes too confused to pay attention to what happens to bodies if and when patients are lost. For a variety of reasons, doctors and nurses, although aware of the critical need for organs, are reluctant to bring up the matter to a family suddenly confronted with a tragic loss. And even when these obstacles are avoided, and the donor cards have been properly filled out, families are likely to continue to withhold approval, for the idea often seems ghoulish when the reality of the death of a loved one is suddenly thrust upon them.

(This shortage of organs does not occur in European countries, where the law works in reverse. Bodies are automatically made available for transplantation, unless the person has previously objected to it—in writing. Can such a law be instituted in this country? Would it violate our civil liberties?)

There is a computerized information bank that catalogs available organs, but it is so slow and antiquated that because of the critical time factor (kidneys can be preserved for 72 hours outside the body, hearts and livers for less than four hours), often when organs are finally located and listed they are no longer usable. Organ procurement centers are at the mercy of commercial airline schedules or the sporadic use of corporate jets. Obviously, this leads to serious and unfortunate logistical problems. Recently, after waiting two weeks for a liver to transplant into a child from San Antonio, Texas, six livers were suddenly available to surgeons in Pittsburgh. Because there are only a few surgical teams with the capability of performing such a delicate and tedious operation, four of those livers went to waste.

If possible, I will be with Denny and his surgical team when they rush cross country in a mad scramble to obtain the twin organs required for Kimberly's delicate operation.

III.   *Immediate Postsurgical Period*

Supersurgeon

Chances of a transplant patient losing life during surgery, especially under the skilled and practiced hands of Dr. Thomas E. Starzl, are slim. It is the hours and days immediately following the surgery, when the patient is susceptible to so many complications and infections, that are so dangerous. During this time, Starzl, the most prominent transplant surgeon in the world, is an ever-looming presence in the hospital.

"He has a red flannel sleeping bag in his office, and when he is exhausted, he puts on a pair of blinders and climbs inside," says Donna Rinaldo. "In an emergency, the nurses pin a note onto the bag and pray that he will see it."

"He has a new wife and two children from a previous marriage," says a co-worker. "God knows when he ever sees them. His only recreation is walking his dog."

It is Thomas Starzl who developed the liver transplantation techniques used so successfully in surgery today, and Starzl is one of two surgeons in the world permitted to experiment with Cyclosporine, the antirejection drug credited with reviving the field of transplantation after its demise in the early seventies. In an article in the August 1984 issue of the *New England Journal of Medicine* (one of more than 600 books and articles he has published during the past two decades) Starzl revealed his newly developed "Pittsburgh Method" of pancreas transplantation, which simplifies surgery and reduces the recovery period by months.

One of the patients on whom I will focus for *The Replaceable Body* may well be the subject of the first bowel transplant in the history of medicine. Starzl expects to attempt such an operation within the year.

It is impossible to spend any time with Thomas Starzl and not be overwhelmed by his energy, his endurance, and his sense of purpose, and awestruck by his charismatic influence over people. Starzl does not walk the corridor of the hospital; he runs. He refuses to wait for elevators; he leaps stairways three steps at a time. During rounds, he will recite a patient's medical history without consulting the chart; he will know the first names of members of the patients' families, and charm them with a flashing smile and piercing eyes of concern. I have personally witnessed embarrassing scenes: patients greeting him with tears of joy, hailing him as their "savior," a man "who has done so much." He is also a favored physician of political leaders and royalty from across the world, and has secretly performed transplants at Presby on four members of the royal family of Saudi Arabia. Recently, King Fahd contributed $400,000 to the transplantation program.

But neither is Starzl a man without imperfections. At 55, he has become a junk food addict and a chain smoker, consuming three packs of cigarettes a day. Reportedly, he has difficulty delegating authority. Whereas the heart transplant unit supervised by Bahnson is as smooth-running and efficient as the heart itself, the liver unit (10-3) over which Starzl presides seems to be administered in a cumbersome manner, with a disorganized staff and sometimes disabled chain of command.

Tough Times on 10-3

Unit 10-3 is composed of two attending physicians, Starzl and an associate from Japan, Shunzaburo Iwatsuki, a number of assisting surgeons and physicians, groups of second- and third-year residents, and, at this particular time, three surgeons in training from Greece. During one recent week, 12 kidney-transplant, two pancreas-transplant, and five liver-transplant patients (there are two additional units, for kidney and heart transplants, on other floors) have been transferred to 10-3 from the Intensive Care Unit for recovery. At full strength, the staff, supervised by Head Nurse Lauren Naughtmann, consists of seven RNs and two aides (daytime) and three RNs for evening shifts. According to the nurses, this is not enough.

At the therapy session conducted each Thursday by Donna Rinaldo, the nurses rattled off their complaints. There were stories about patients being returned to the unit from the operating room still bleeding, of arguments between doctors over prescribed treatment, sometimes in front of the patients, and something especially frustrating to nurses (and also frustrating to many of the other surgeons): the unfailing loyalty of the patients to Tom Starzl.

"These people suffer from a 'Starzl is God' syndrome," one nurse said.

The dissatisfaction on 10-3 is not caused completely by Starzl, or any particular person or incident, according to Naughtmann. It is the never-relenting pressure of having to deal with people constantly lying in the no man's land between life and death.

"Sometimes I just can't smile at them anymore," one nurse explained. "My head is pounding and my stomach is on fire."

"So why do you stay?"

"Because I can't bear the thought of what might happen to them without me."

IV.   Rejection

Shattered Hope

There are almost always setbacks, usually only minor infections that delay recovery by a few days, perhaps a week, but because of the delicate nature of the operation and the weakened condition of the patient after years of failing health, there are also serious and frequent complications. Here are a few examples of the people currently or recently in residence in Unit 10-3 and the problems they have had to confront:

Joyce Howard, 48, received a liver transplant on April 20, but contracted herpes as soon as she got home, and had to return to the unit.

Guan Ho Chen, an aide to the Prince of Bhutan, had a liver transplant in December 1983, but because he lives three days over land from the nearest airport, he has had to remain in Pittsburgh indefinitely.

Michael Silliman was the victim of a stroke, while recuperating from a second liver transplant (the first rejected).

Tabor Phillips, a nurse from Arizona, was admitted on March 3, received a transplant on April 9, but was forced to remain at the hospital indefinitely because of a continuing build-up of fluids in her lungs.

Rebecca Hardesty, a 26-year-old grade school teacher from New Jersey, waited six months in a trailer near Pittsburgh, until she was summoned for a liver transplant. When doctors opened her up, they discovered cancer. She returned home . . . to die.

Gerard Patterson, 42, received a kidney last summer, and then, a few months later, a pancreas transplant. At home he contracted an ulcer on his foot, which became infected. He did not tell his doctors for fear of having to undergo another operation. Last week, Patterson's leg was amputated.

"When Gerard lost his leg, the whole place seemed to collapse for a while," said Lauren Naughtmann. "All of us, doctors, residents, nurses, aides, it made us all sick." Ray Blasingame and Jerry Blanford did not suffer through a first rejection period. Hopefully, Kimberly Fuller will be blessed with similar good fortune.

V.   Recovery Period

Family House

It is three long blocks down (and up) what students for generations have called "Cardiac Hill" to the newly renovated three-story Victorian structure known as "Family House," established two years ago for patients waiting for organs and for families waiting for fathers, wives, children to progress through the seemingly unending transplantation process. Seventy-five people squeezed sometimes four in a room, sharing a community kitchen and one large color TV, with a list of 75 more, waiting for admittance. Residents of Family House come from every corner of the world, and from vastly different cultural and economic situations, but together they share problems no one else could understand.

"This experience has separated us from everyday living," says Hazel Blasingame, Ray's mother, a resident of Family House for nearly six months, "and brought our world to an indefinite standstill. We are not productive. We don't have a daily routine. We no longer permit ourselves to consider the possibility of a future. It's a gruesome atmosphere here, waiting for an organ. First you wonder if your son will be one of the fortunate five percent chosen, and once he's chosen, you wonder why he was one of the few to be saved."

Social worker Donna Rinaldo conducts a regular therapy group at Family House each Thursday, and the Reverend Leslie Reimer, a special pastor assigned by the Episcopal Diocese in Pittsburgh to the transplant units at Presby, makes frequent visits.

"One lady has been a transplant patient for 155 days, and she's lived and suffered through every kind of physical and emotional complication imaginable. But during all that time, a family member, living at Family House, has been constantly with her. When her husband ran out of vacation days, the family set up a 24-hour rotation from home, to Family House, to hospital. Even the doctors admit . . . it is the faith and commitment of the family that is keeping her alive."

This same family, says Reverend Reimer, is soon to face the most serious setback of all. They are almost out of money and credit. The maximum allowed through their Major Medical coverage—$250,000— will soon be exceeded. "Their house is already mortgaged to the hilt. They don't know what to do."

From Family House to White House

Reimer is extremely concerned with the financial and ethical issues surrounding transplantation. "In a world where people die from lack of basic health care, and necessities like food and common drugs, what is the place of transplantation? Resources expended on transplantation include not only money and intellect, but also blood, operating room space and time, beds and staff, and the human energy consumed both in transplant surgery itself and the pre- and post-operative care of patients."

Previously, most of the funds for experimental transplantation were generated from private foundations and government grants. But who will pay the price now that transplantation is beginning to receive wide acceptance? As the controversial Governor Lamm of Colorado recently asked: How much is too much to save a life?

Over the past few years, Nancy and Ronald Reagan have made a number of radio and television appeals for donors to aid people, mostly children, in their quest for complicated transplant operations. President Reagan has also appointed a White House staff assistant, Michael E.

Batten, as his personal liaison between hospitals and state and private insurance agencies battling over the issue of transplantation and coverage. To date, Batten has aided in saving more than 400 lives through personal intervention, including that of Jerry Blanford, whose private insurance company refused to put up the $200,000 cash deposit required by Presby—until the morning after Michael Batten read Blanford's letter and picked up the phone.

More Media Magic

Both Blasingame and Blanford have each received an additional $50,000 for care and treatment from hometown newspaper campaigns. Also, Reagan has recently agreed to do a series of TV spots at Presby, for all Westinghouse Broadcasting Co. affiliate stations, focusing on the critical need for organ donors. But many Democrats consider Reagan's interest in transplantation a "media scam" designed to stimulate a steady stream of heartrending publicity events for a president running for re-election. If Reagan were sincerely concerned, they say, he would sponsor legislation to help all the sick and the poor—not just the people requiring organ transplantation.

Upon returning home from Presby, after Kimberly's evaluation, Sandy Fuller wrote Ronald Reagan and Michael Batten long letters, asking for help. "It isn't the ultimate solution to our problem," said Reverend Reimer, "but right now it's the only solution we've got."

VI. Discharge

Is Life After Transplantation Worth Living?

As I follow a transplant patient through the stages of evaluation, surgery, and recovery, I will also be following discharged transplant recipients as they attempt to rebuild their lives. Is a normal life possible for organ recipients? The answer is yes—at least from a physical standpoint. But will recipients be permitted by society to live a normal life?

First, there is the critical question of Cyclosporine, the drug that prevents bodies from rejecting transplanted organs. Transplant recipients must take Cyclosporine for the rest of their lives.

As Dr. Starzl explained to a House of Representatives subcommittee, Cyclosporine was originally considered experimental, and thus it was provided free by the manufacturer, Sandoz, to all transplant recipients. Now that it is FDA approved, recipients must pay—an expense of anywhere from $5,000 to $10,000 annually. Most health insurance policies (including Medicare) will not cover the total cost of Cyclosporine. And because they have been sick for so long, many recipients cannot obtain health insurance at all.

Medical science has provided organ recipients with new life contingent upon the inescapable habit of Cyclosporine, which they cannot afford. And, as transplantation centers continue to open throughout the nation, tens of thousands of "Cyclosporine junkies" will be created annually, men and women presented with the gift of life without the means to live it.

It is likely that the Cyclosporine issue will be resolved (Congress seems to be moving in that direction), but the stigma of being a transplant recipient will probably not go away so quickly. Members of TRIO (Transplant Recipients International Organization) report that they are finding it increasingly difficult to locate full-time employment. It is a vicious circle. Large companies will not hire them because insurance carriers will not cover transplant recipients. A few small companies will employ transplant recipients, but prospects for responsible positions across the United States are currently very dim.

But *The Replaceable Body* will not be a story with an unhappy ending. Not when readers see Terri Lenz at home, happy, caring for her children. Jerry Blanford has also returned to Illinois, now a son with two loving mothers, corresponding with a Hollywood movie producer interested in recreating the story of his life. Although Ray Blasingame must stay in Pittsburgh indefinitely, he is planning to register for night school to earn his high school diploma.

The coming weeks and months may be clouded by the uncertainty caused by their status as recent transplant recipients and the difficult task of starting over, but for the first time in a long time, Ray, Jerry, and Terri are secure in the knowledge that the future is filled with exciting potential. Life is no longer a fading possibility. It is reality, rich with hope and promise.

Appendix 2

On the Road to an M.F.A.

Not too long ago, the concept of studying writing in a "creative writing program" was unheard of. If you wanted to be a writer, then you became an avid reader and a citizen of the world, learning about life through travel and personal experience until you knew enough to write an essay, short story, or poem that said something. In college, you majored in English literature, philosophy, or history—areas of concentration that would introduce the best books and the most influential thinkers. Even today in countries outside of the United States, creative writing programs on a high school or university level are literally nonexistent.

There are approximately 300 creative writing programs to choose from nationwide, beginning with the program at the University of Iowa in Iowa City, which is the oldest and considered to be one of the best. You can get an undergraduate (Bachelor of Arts) degree in creative writing, as well as a graduate (Master of Arts) degree.

Probably the best graduate degree in writing is an M.F.A.—a Master of Fine Arts—essentially the same advanced level and calibre of degree that musicians, directors, or visual artists earn. A few colleges even offer a Ph.D. in creative writing, primarily for people who prefer to teach rather than to write.

Creative writing programs, especially on the graduate level, require students to major or specialize in one genre: fiction, nonfiction, or poetry, and a few in creative nonfiction. Listed in the back of this book are low residency programs that allow writers to remain at home through most of the year and work with a writing instructor through the mail and by fax and telephone, and ask just a two-week on-campus residency.

Undergraduate students interested in nonfiction most often will either major in journalism with a minor in a field such as history, political science, economics, or literature, or they will do the opposite—major in an outside area while minoring in writing. Students should think seriously about majoring in the sciences, which are becoming increasingly difficult to understand; many jobs will be available for people who can write strong prose that explains medicine, engineering, physics, and so forth.

Creative writing programs bring together people from throughout the United States and provide a sense of community to those students who feel a special kinship and dedication to the written word. Being a writer can be an extremely lonely occupation. Poet and essayist Diane Ackerman, author of *A Natural History of the Senses*, remembers that her teachers in high school were so opposed to her writing that she concealed her journals, and her dreams about being a writer, until her second year in college.

I especially like creative writing programs on a graduate level because of the final requirement: In most programs a student must complete a book-length manuscript. Consequently, you will have written your first book before you graduate—with the help of your teachers. It is the consummate experience for student writers, and the last time they will receive such guidance and support.

The M.F.A. degree is also a good credential for a teaching position in a creative writing program, although most creative writing programs on a university level prefer people with strong publishing credits (books, essays in important magazines) whether they have a degree or not; but an M.F.A. is an extra plus.

Having said all of that I should also point out that most of the great American writers were not educated in creative writing programs. Ernest Hemingway never even attended a university, for example. After graduating high school, he became an ambulance driver for the Italian army during World War I and observed combat firsthand. He was seriously wounded in the process, an experience that led to some of his finest work.

I, too, am not a product of a writing program; while driving a beer-delivery truck and selling shoes, I majored in liberal arts. I do not have a master's degree, although I am a tenured professor at the University of Pittsburgh.

Whether you choose writing programs, other majors, or the College of Hard Knocks, the proof of your work is not measured by a degree you receive on paper, but rather by the images you create and the ideas you communicate on paper. My professorial position came as a result of my accomplishments as a creative nonfiction writer and not because of any degree.

No matter how and where you expect to go in the future, being able to write will be a considerable advantage. The experience gained in learning to deal with people and adjusting to other ways of life—a primary challenge in an immersion—will be equally valuable.

Appendix 3

Writers' Colonies and Conferences

You are sitting in a cozy log cabin, nestled in the New England woods, and you are writing. It is a cool fall morning, but a warm fire is crackling on the hearth. Hungry? Open the front door; a wicker basket with sandwiches and a container of hot vegetable soup has been placed on the porch. You nibble on the sandwich and sip the soup in the sun before returning to your cabin for a few more hours of writing.

Later that day, you canoe across the lake next to your cabin or simply wander into a nearby meadow to read and nap in the sun.

Somewhere around dusk, there's a cocktail hour in the main building, and suddenly this deserted country encampment is filled with a dozen or more creative and interesting people: writers, painters, sculptors, composers; sipping wine or soda and discussing their day. Dinner is served. The interesting conversation continues for some people, while others return to their rooms in the inn or their studios in the woods to work.

Every day, the same pattern takes shape. You and all the other residents do whatever you choose to do: write, paint, swim, sleep. Whatever makes you happy. You may stay a month or three months. Here at this artists' colony, one of several dozen colonies across the United States, artists are treated as royalty. Every effort is made by your hosts to make life pleasant.

I have been a guest at a couple of artists' colonies for month-long residencies, one in Virginia at the Virginia Center for Creative Arts and another at a phenomenal place called Yaddo, a 19th-century mansion and 200-acre estate in Saratoga Springs, New York.

As you can imagine, this is a great life to lead, truly a joy to discover. And the best part of the entire experience at an artists' colony is that many of them are free.

Not that admission is easy. One must apply and competition is stiff, although writers in the early stages of their careers who show talent and maturity often are accepted.

There are also summer writers' conferences to attend as a student or faculty member: intense times (some are weekends, some as long as two weeks) of conversation and workshops and seminars about all genres of writing with like-minded people. The first and only writers' conference specializing exclusively in creative nonfiction is co-sponsored by *Creative Nonfiction* and takes place annually at Goucher College in Baltimore. Information can be obtained by calling 1-800-697-4646.

Appendix 4

Helpful Information

Reference Books and Organizations Creative Nonfiction Writers Should Know About

"Grants and Awards Available to American Writers"
PEN American Center
568 Broadway
New York, NY 10012

Directory of Literary Magazines
Council of Literary Magazines and Presses
154 Christopher Street, Suite 3C
New York, NY 10014

The Associated Press Stylebook and Libel Manual
Addision-Wesley Publishing Co., Inc.
Jacob Way
Reading, MA 01867

Low Residency and Nonfiction M.F.A. Programs and
On Cloud Nine: Writers' Colonies, Retreats, Ranches, Residencies, and Sanctuaries
Poets & Writers, Inc.
72 Spring Street
New York, NY 10012

Writers' Market: Where and How to Sell What You Write
1507 Dana Avenue
Cincinnati, OH 45207

National Association of Science Writers, Inc.
P.O. Box 294
Greenlawn, NY 11740

American Society of Journalists and Authors
1501 Broadway, Suite 302
New York, NY 10036

Associated Writing Programs
George Mason University
Fairfax, VA

Works of Authorship: A Guide to Understanding Copyrights
Buchanan Ingersoll P.C.
412-562-8800

Writers' Conferences and Festivals
P.O. Box 102396
Denver, CO 80250

Reading List

For regular information about the writing community:

Poets & Writers Magazine
72 Spring Street
New York, NY 10012

For essays and profiles of the finest creative nonfiction writers:

Creative Nonfiction
P.O. Box 81536
Pittsburgh, PA 15217

Creative Nonfiction Reading List: A Random Recommended Selection of Books and Authors to Sample and Enjoy, from the Editors of the Journal Creative Nonfiction:

Anthologies

The Art of the Personal Essay, with an introduction by Philip Lopate

Best American Essays, edited by Robert Atwan

The Creative Nonfiction Reader, edited by Lee Gutkind

The John McPhee Reader, with an introduction by William Haworth

The Second John McPhee Reader, with an introduction by David Remnick

Suggested Books and Authors

Desert Solitaire, Edward Abbey

Remembering Heaven's Face, John Balaban

Loving Rachel, Jane Bernstein

Bringing the Heat, Mark Bowden

Friendly Fire, C. D. B. Bryan

The Corpse Had a Familiar Face, Edna Buchanan

In Cold Blood, Truman Capote

The White Album, Joan Didion

Pilgrim at Tinker Creek, Annie Dillard

This House of Sky, Ivan Doig

The Broken Cord, Michael Dorris

The Studio, John Gregory Dunne

The Great Plains, Ian Frasier

The Last Shot, Darcy Frey

Colored People, Henry Louis Gates

The Shadow Man, Mary Gordon

Stuck in Time, Lee Gutkind

Blue Highways, William Least Heat-Moon

Dispatches, Michael Herr

All Creatures Great and Small, James Herriot

Hiroshima, John Hersey

Far-Flung Hubbell, Sue Hubbell

Liar's Club, Mary Karr

House, Tracy Kidder

Not Necessarily a Benign Procedure, Perri Klass

There Are No Children Here, Alex Kotlowitz

Cowboy, Jane Kramer

Invasive Procedures, Mark Kramer

The Balloon Lady and Other People I Know, Jeanne Marie Laskas

Hunting the Whole Way Home, Sidney Lea

Arctic Dreams, Barry Lopez

Common Ground, J. Anthony Lukas

The Executioner's Song, Norman Mailer

The Journalist and the Murderer, Janet Malcolm

The Snow Leopard, Peter Matthiessen

Mornings on Horseback, David McCullough

Fatal Vision, Joe McGinniss

Up in the Old Hotel, Joseph Mitchell

The Lost Childhood, Yehuda Nir

The Hottest Water in Chicago: Notes of a Native Daughter, Gayle Pemberton

Zen and the Art of Motorcycle Maintenance, Robert M. Pirsig

Paper Lion, George Plimpton

Second Nature, Michael Pollan

Mr. Personality, Mark Singer

Travels With Charlie, John Steinbeck

Fame and Obscurity, Gay Talese

Lives of a Cell, Lewis Thomas

Hell's Angels, Hunter S. Thompson

Killings, Calvin Trillin

Assorted Prose, John Updike

My Own Country, A Doctor's Story, Abraham Verghese

The Onion Field, Joseph Wambaugh

One Writer's Beginnings, Eudora Welty

Brothers and Keepers, John Wideman

Night, Eli Wiesel

The Right Stuff, Tom Wolfe

This Boy's Life, Tobias Wolff

All the President's Men, Bob Woodward and Carl Bernstein

Appendix 5

Readings

"The Incident"

BY LEE GUTKIND*
(CHAPTER 1)

When I drove up to the house, Daniel was walking toward me. I got out of the car and waited for him to approach. Even though he waved and flashed a quick smile, he seemed grim and befuddled. "What's wrong, Dan?"

He shrugged and shook his head as we walked up the steps toward the porch. "Nothing's wrong," he said, but his eyes were darting erratically from side to side.

Daniel had been working periodically that summer at a rental property I owned, cleaning out the basement, a filthy job that he savored. Nothing made Daniel happier than getting dirty, especially with a bunch of junk. A pack rat, Daniel had always rummaged through trash, rescuing an array of worthless mechanical objects—manual typewriters, speedometers, radios, lamps, rusty tools, old motors. Keys of any size, type, or condition were his special passion, and locks, whether or not they corresponded to the keys. Sometimes he managed to clean or fix a derelict item of junk and sell it at a Sunday flea market, but usually

*From Lee Gutkind, *Stuck in Time: The Tragedy of Childhood Mental Illness,* © 1993. Reprinted with permission of Henry Holt and Company, Inc.

Daniel was more interested in contemplating these items in the questionable safety of his room.

Daniel is short and broad, part muscle from his recent forays into weight lifting and part paunch from overeating. It was not unusual for him to devour an entire large pizza with mushrooms, sausage, and pepperoni—our traditional Saturday-afternoon snack—followed by a few hot sausage hoagies for dinner. Over the past three years, he had changed a good deal physically; when he was twelve, he weighed ninety pounds, a frail and exceedingly delicate feather of a boy; now, still very short, he could be more aptly described as a fireplug.

We stopped at the top of the steps, and I put my hands on his shoulders. Ruffling his curly hair with my hand, I joked about how dirty he was and made a crack about his ears, which are unusually small. I could almost always get him to laugh by invoking his ears or by pointing out that he was most handsome on Halloween, when he wore a mask. But this time he did not laugh, or protest; he was so somber that I pulled him down on the stoop and looked him straight in the eye. "C'mon, Dan. Something's wrong. What's going on?"

Although I could see it coming, I was surprised at the power of his emotions. A mask of fear suddenly exploded onto his face, and he began to whine, like a small, frightened child. "Oh, I'm so scared," he said. "He's going to kill me."

His eyes darted crazily, and he tried to stand up and run, but I held on to him. "I won't let anyone hurt you."

Tears were streaming down his face, which he buried in my chest. "A man molested me." He reached down and began squeezing his buttocks. "Oh, it hurts," he wailed. "It hurts so bad back there."

Daniel poured out his story in the midst of choking sobs. He had worked in the basement for half an hour or so, dragging out a mess of discarded timber, empty paint cans, and old furniture, and then decided to take a five-minute walk to the local convenience store for a soda. There's a bank of pay phones on the corner beside the store, and as he was passing, a phone was ringing. Daniel answered. A male voice at the other end said that he had been waiting for Daniel and would kill him if he didn't do what he was told. "Yeah, sure," Daniel had replied, hanging up the phone and going to the store.

But when Daniel walked past the telephones on his return, a car screeched to a halt at the curb. A man, unshaven, dressed in black trousers and shirt and black patent leather shoes and waving a knife, ordered Daniel inside. Instead of running, or screaming—or even laughing—Daniel complied. They drove around the corner, down a side street, and into an alley, whereupon the man led Daniel through a clump of bushes behind an abandoned building. Following orders, Daniel kissed the man on the lips, then under the threat of the knife, sank to his knees and performed oral sex. Finally, Daniel lay facedown on the ground. The man entered him. Daniel felt a sharp and intrusive pain. Now, at the end of the story, Daniel was nearly hysterical. "Oh, it hurts so bad. He said he'd kill me if I told anyone. What am I going to do?"

I could not answer his question, for I felt dumbfounded and conflicted. This incident had occurred in my neighborhood, an area in which I lived with my wife and infant son, and one considered the most urbane in the city. Not that crime never occurred here, but child molestation (or kidnapping) in the middle of a bright and busy Saturday afternoon was unlikely, to say the least.

Besides, there was Daniel's history to consider, beginning with the abuse and neglect that had led authorities to permanently separate Daniel from his family when he was ten years old. The abuse during his early years had been documented, but recently, new and questionable incidents of violence and molestation had allegedly occurred. Only a couple of weeks ago, Daniel had come home with his face bruised and his books and wallet missing. He claimed to have been attacked by four black kids, wielding pipes, who stole his money and beat him up. Later, witnesses reported that he had actually gotten into a fight with a neighborhood kid, who was white—and lost.

Last year, Daniel had reported that a teenage female resident of his group home had accosted him in a darkened passageway and molested him. At about the same time, Daniel told a convoluted story about being followed by a mysterious bearded man who had forced him into his Cadillac and molested him. Daniel also claimed that a teacher at school was abusing him and encouraging him to run away and not attend classes.

Many of the past horrors in Daniel's life had been confirmed, but his recent credibility was partially suspect because of his own maliciousness. Hadn't he, one Saturday afternoon, removed all the manhole covers from the sewer system on the periphery of his group home and covered the holes with twigs, grass, and weeds as "booby traps?" Hadn't he promised, after I had explained the danger, to immediately replace the manhole covers, and hadn't he reneged on that promise? Didn't he lie frequently about where he went and what he did, using his learning disabilities and side effects from antidepressant medication as justifications for forgetting and making mistakes?

Some of his excuses were plausible, especially those attributed to his learning disabilities. The intent of messages directed toward him sometimes did not register, but because Daniel was intuitive and responsive, he skillfully maintained eye contact with the person to whom he was speaking, able to sense when to shake his head, shrug, or nod, indicating understanding while completely in the dark. But there was an unpredictable side to Daniel, as well; he was a kid who tottered on the precarious edge of ambiguity.

The "booby trap" incident had been especially disturbing because it made me realize that Daniel's defensiveness could distort his sense of right and wrong. The caseworker at his group home observed that Daniel had been so brutally battered by his family and by the child welfare system that "rescued" him that it was impossible for him to feel compassion. The fact that someone could have been hurt—or killed—by his "booby traps" meant little to Daniel, who frequently declared, "I don't care about anyone else."

I don't believe that Daniel wants to hurt anyone, but because of his history, he possesses an irrational and uncontrollable fear of being taken advantage of, especially by someone unknown. This helps to explain his penchant for locks, keys, and burglar alarms, and suspicions toward strangers. Daniel could have seen this unshaven man dressed in black sitting in his car or making a telephone call and his imagination might have done the rest.

Daniel continued to whimper as I tried to decide how to proceed. At the very least, I had to get him away from this house and the fear that the mysterious man, whether real or imagined, was going to come back for him. I remembered a story he'd told me of another unshaven man who lived in the woods across from his home who would periodically sneak into the room he occupied with his sister—and molest them both. The power of his emotions and the horror of what might have happened to him confused and frightened me. Hurriedly, we gathered his possessions and climbed into my car.

I drove in the general direction of the convenience store until Daniel pointed to the street to which the man had taken him. Instinctively, I turned the corner. Daniel directed me into the alley he had described. For the first time, I began to believe that the incident could have happened. The alley was not dark or narrow, but it was clearly out of the way, as was the building to which he pointed, set off in a secluded corner of a vacant lot. The underbrush around the building was thick and concealing. If a molestation had occurred, it could have happened here.

I backed down the alley and once again headed for the store. A police van was sitting in the parking lot, its engines idling. Out of the corner of my eye, I could see two officers, both women, eating a take-out lunch and listening to their walkie-talkie. Daniel was staring straight ahead, whimpering and snuffling. He did not see the police van, but its presence provided a direction—right or wrong.

"Well, Dan, this is your chance," I said, pointing at the white van with its large blue-and-gold official seal. "We could approach those officers and tell them what happened."

Daniel did not hesitate. "Yes," he said, with conviction. Daniel has always possessed an irrepressible penchant for law enforcement officers, which is what he wanted to become. The order and control that police may establish appeals to kids who have lacked the order and control which might have made their lives happier and safer. As Daniel had grown older, the idea of being a policeman had faded, although their uniforms and authority were still quite seductive.

We got out of the car, walked across the parking lot, and knocked on the window of the van. "I was molested by a man dressed in black," Daniel said. He quickly highlighted the gruesome details.

Almost instantly, the officer on the driver's side activated her walkie-talkie. Announcing the specific location, I heard her summarize Daniel's story to her sergeant, using the word that both Daniel and I had studiously avoided: "A reported rape . . ."

Within five minutes, the entire parking lot was ringed with police vehicles. Daniel was asked to tell his story twice more, once by a sergeant and then by a medic, and with each telling Daniel became more distraught. He buried his face in my chest and began sobbing uncontrollably, especially when the medic attempted to take him in the ambulance to the hospital for the long and intense physical examination required.

"Lee, you have to come with me; I don't want to be alone."

"You go in the ambulance, Dan. I'll be along in my own car. Don't worry, I won't leave you."

When I arrived at the emergency room a few minutes later, the police would not permit me to join him in the examination room. Daniel remained alone with the doctors, nurses, and policemen for the next six hours. As directed, I went home and sat by the telephone, waiting for the police to contact me. I did not know what to believe—or even what I wanted to believe. Did I want the police to determine that Daniel was telling the truth—that he had really been raped? Or would it be preferable to learn that Daniel had been lying or hallucinating? Either way, Daniel was the ultimate victim—of society, his family, his biology, and of himself.

Late that autumn afternoon, I led two police officers back to the scene of the alleged molestation—the place to which Daniel had initially directed me. Daniel had told the police that the man had dragged him through the thick underbrush surrounding the abandoned building and molested him behind it. But the weeds and bushes revealed no sign of being trampled or disturbed, and later, the tests conducted by the hospital doctor were inconclusive. There were definite traces of semen on Daniel's shirt, but there was no evidence of penetration. Daniel could not explain to the doctor, the nurses, or the police investigators why he answered the telephone while walking toward the convenience store—or why he entered the man's car when he could have run in any direction, screaming for help.

During the following few weeks, the more people doubted and questioned the details and the logic of his experience, the more Daniel proclaimed its accuracy. "You may not believe me, and my mother may not believe, and the police may not believe me," he told me, "but I know what happened. I don't care what anybody says. The man molested me. You don't know anything about it."

Daniel was right. I didn't know anything about it, and I guess the truth of the matter is that I really didn't want to. The situation was too perplexing and too painful to dwell upon. Whether the rape had actually occurred or whether the entire incident was a creation of his own imagination, I have come to believe that it was a signal from Daniel—a cry for attention, help, and understanding to anyone who might listen. He felt himself slipping. Emotionally, he was circling the drain.

Rape constituted the loudest symbolic scream he could yell. And he had been partially successful. He had attracted the attention of the police, with whom he most desired contact, his mother, his big brother, his caseworker—all of the people in his life. We had all stopped dead in our tracks to look and to listen and to respond to Daniel, to be there for him during a brief time of need. But when the immediate crisis was over, the investigation completed and the new work week started, everyone had returned to his or her own personal preoccupations. Daniel was still screaming for help, but we no longer had the time or the patience to listen. He was screaming into his future, which was as empty as his past.

"Teeth"
BY LEE GUTKIND*

After breakfast, her husband looked up from across the table and announced that he was taking her into town to have all her teeth pulled out. It took a while for the meaning of his words to penetrate. Even when he said he was getting her a new set of teeth, she stared at him blankly. The memory of that morning nearly six months ago, pained her even now.

"My teeth ain't perfect, but they never give me or my husband no trouble," she said, rolling her eyes and shaking her head back and forth

From Lee Gutkind, *The People of Penns Woods West*, © 1984. Reprinted by permission of the University of Pittsburgh Press.

slowly. "And suddenly, there he wanted to go and pull them all out. I've never been so surprised in all my life."

She was sitting on a stoop in front of the tarpaper-covered cabin in which she and her husband lived, petting the old coon dog, curled in a grimy heap at her feet, and watching the tractor-trailer trucks whoosh by. Each time a truck went up the road, she would wave and smile. The truckers would invariably wave back, as they roared by, bellowing smoke.

She told me that her loneliness was sometimes awful. It wasn't the mountains—she had lived here all her life and wasn't interested in anywhere else—but the fact that no one was around to talk to. The gloomy shadow that fell across her face blatantly telegraphed her desperation. Each time I visited, she went on and on, could hardly stop herself from talking.

She was a river of fat. Her body bulged and rippled in every direction, and her eyes, tucked into her pasty skin, looked like raisins pressed into cookie dough. Her hair was dirty gray, tangled and wooly, but you could tell her face had once been pretty. When she showed me her picture as an infant, I remarked that she looked like the Ivory Snow baby. Blushing, she covered her mouth and turned away. That was how we had first got on the subject of her teeth.

One day in town her husband was approached by the new dentist, a handsome young man in a white shirt and a blue and red striped tie, who explained that his house needed a new roof. Would he be interested in installing it in return for money or services?

Her husband was a short, wiry old man of seventy-two, who resembled a chicken hawk, with a hooked nose and arms that bowed out like furled wings. He hunched forward when he walked, as if he were about to take off flying. He told the dentist he would think on it for a while.

That evening, after supper, he stooped down and peered into her mouth, testing each of her teeth with his thumb and forefinger to see how well they were rooted. "Smile," he told her. "Laugh." She followed his instructions to the letter, as was her habit. Over the next few days, he watched her every chance he got. It was early autumn when he finally went back into town to make the deal. She never knew anything about it.

The woman explained that she and her husband had very little use for cash, bartering for almost everything they needed. They traded vegetables, cultivated on their tiny patch of land, for fruit—corn for peaches, tomatoes for apples, pickles for pears, beets for pretty bluefire plums. He chopped wood in return for mason jars. Periodically, he repaired a car for a guy who owned a dry goods store in town in exchange for clothes for both of them. By bartering instead of buying and selling, they hardly paid Uncle Sam a penny's worth of taxes.

Last summer, he raised a barn for some city folks, recently retired near here, in return for an old engine from a '64 Buick and a side of beef. The engine went into a pickup truck they had gotten for one hundred fifty dozen eggs. Paid out over a period of three months, the eggs came from their chicken coops out back. The pickup was then swapped to the owner of a local filling station for credit for two hundred gallons of gas, plus an assortment of parts and tools. Meanwhile, she boiled up the beef on the old black cast-iron stove that had belonged to his grandfather, and canned and stored most of it in the cold-cellar cave under the house. She cut the remainder of the beef in strips and hung them like wet socks above the stove, smoking and shriveling them down to jerky. From the spring to the fall, her husband went fishing each evening after dinner. When he collected a big batch of trout, she stewed them in the pressure cooker until the whole fish, bones and all, was white and meaty like tuna. This was what they would eat next winter and the winters thereafter. Their cave was stocked with years of stuff.

Her husband never talked about his work and what was owed to him in the way of goods and services, and she never asked. Despite her significant contribution, the actual swapping wasn't her business. Years ago, her daddy had told her in no uncertain terms exactly what she needed to know to get herself through life. He was a man much like her husband, didn't owe anyone and never wasted anything. No words in conversation, unless some specific point was to be made. Otherwise, silence was golden.

One night, however, her father came outside and squeezed down on the stoop beside her. They lived in an old house along the side of the road, about the same size as the one in which she and her husband lived now. But her father only rented it for fifty dollars a month. Neither her father nor his father before him had ever owned a piece of property straight out.

At the time, she didn't know that the old man was dying from cancer. Her mother had also died from cancer, and she had had to quit school in the sixth grade to take care of the rest of the kids and keep house. Recently, her two older brothers had joined the army, while the younger kids were sent to foster homes. Now, she and her father were home alone. She was fifteen at the time.

They sat side by side as the night grew colder. The moon shimmered in the glittering dish of sky, but the air felt like rain. Suddenly he cleared his throat. The sound of his voice made her feel uncomfortable, similar to how she felt trying on a new pair of boots.

"What else is there in life?" He said this as if in summation after a long conversation which she had somehow missed. Then, he paused. She would never forget his face as they sat there. His hard, sharp features seemed to disintegrate in the darkness. The glitter reflecting from the moonlight faded from the blue of his eyes.

"You work to eat, you eat to live, you live to work." He sighed. "That's all there are to it."

The next morning, the man who was soon to become her husband made himself known. Miraculously, all the details had been worked out between the man and her father in advance, without her having the slightest idea of what was happening. The following afternoon, the man came and took her away. Two weeks later, her father died.

She cleared her throat and motioned toward the house with her fat, flesh-soaked arm. "We came right here to these two acres and moved into an old shed out back. It ain't there no more. Tore it down to salvage the wood for this place. First we made sure we had good water, then we started building. From start to finish it took two years to get all set up. The winters were awful, but the summers weren't too bad."

All this happened some thirty years ago. Her husband had been married once before. His first wife died or left him, she wasn't sure, and his children, who she never met, were all grown up and living somewhere in another part of the state. Once in a great while, there was a letter, which he would read carefully, his lips moving, then stuff into his pocket, shaking his head and muttering. He would go on, muttering and cursing, shaking his head, for days at a time, without so much as an explanation.

Her own brothers and sisters all lived near here, but hardly ever stopped by or invited her to visit. Like most everyone else, they were more than a little afraid of her somber, silent husband.

Once again, she paused to wave at a trucker, barreling up the narrow two-lane highway. Their shack had been built unusually close to the asphalt. Even from up in the sleeping loft inside, you could hear the cinders and feel the wind when the trucks rumbled by. She said she was so shocked and angry when she found out about the deal her husband had made with the new dentist that she started screaming and yelling. "I had never acted that way before, but I just couldn't help myself. All of a sudden, I went crazy. My husband didn't know what to do."

He had turned away, glaring in silence out the window. It was still early. The sun was just beginning its ascent up the hill toward them. His eyes narrowed. Time passed as he stared down the road. His brows, thick and hairy, cast a shadow, like umbrellas over his eyelids. When the sunlight reached up as far as their house, he got up and finished dressing. He bit off a plug of tobacco, stuffed it under his cheek, put on his old grimy baseball cap, climbed into his pickup, and turned her over. When he saw his wife come out onto the porch, he threw the truck into reverse, backed up, and leaned out the window. He wanted to have his say one more time. "We shook hands on a new set of teeth. It's owed to me."

She turned and walked back into the house without a word. He peeled out onto the asphalt, his tires spitting gravel.

In no time, her best clothes were out of the drawer and piled on the bed. She found an old suitcase, cleaned it inside and out carefully, before laying in her clothes. The last time she had been on any sort of trip was when her husband had come to take her from her daddy. They didn't have a suitcase then. All her possessions, including her mother's big black roasting pan, fit easily into a medium-sized cardboard box. Her father carried the box down to the road and they waited together until the man who was to become her husband arrived. The whole thing—packing, waiting, and driving away—all took about ten minutes. It went by in a blur, one moment stacked up on top of another.

Thinking back, she realized that her life had ended right about then. She had been isolated with this man who hardly talked to her and whom she hardly knew, a man who had refused to discuss his past for over thirty years. At least with her father there was evidence of some roots and another life somewhere behind the one he had been living. But this man's world was bleak, both behind and beyond. He offered little more than a nod or a grunt for sustenance each day. Her father's words, uttered with such sadness and resignation on that damp, dark night so many centuries ago, came back to her now. You work to eat, you eat to live, you live to work. That's all there are to it.

All right. She had lived her life in accordance with her father's wishes, had never asked for anything from anyone, never shirked her responsibilities or wasted a breath. She had always done whatever her husband had told her to do—and more. But giving up a part of her own body simply for the sake of a business deal was too much. It was going too far. A person has a God-given right to own certain things, especially when they were born with it.

The last thing she did before leaving was to go out to the pump house and peer into the mirror. The image she saw glaring back at her was awful. She was too old, too fat, and too dirty. But, if anything, her face had held up best of all. There was still a spark, a hint of the beauty that might have been.

Her daddy, who never had more than a dollar in his pocket at any one time, had always bragged that the Good Lord had made him rich by blessing him with a daughter with a millon-dollar smile. Even now, she could hear the distant echo of his praise. She wasn't going to let that damn bastard she married squash the memory by pulling out her teeth.

She looked up at me. The shroud that had fallen over her face as she told her story momentarily lifted. "Used to be my husband would leave me alone from early morning until supper. But now, things is different. He's liable to ride by anytime, just to check and see if I'm still here. Sometimes I hide out behind the chicken coops and wait for him. When the house looks empty, he'll stop to see where I am. He always pretends he's come back for tools or materials, but I know I got him worried. It serves him right."

She dug her fingers into her scalp, shook her head vehemently, scratching simultaneously before continuing. "I left the house that morning, hitchhiked into town, and bought a ticket for Davenport, Iowa. Davenport was the only city in the state I could think of. My daddy traveled all over the country when he was younger. He told me you could drive for half a day in any one direction in Iowa and not see anything else but a green carpet of corn, just bending and stretching in the distance."

She pushed her big blubbery legs out into the grass, right near where the old coon dog was lying. Once in a while, the dog would thrash around and thump its tail against the ground. A couple of times, it pushed itself up and crawled over on top of us. The woman had on brown doubleknit slacks worn through at the knees. Her blouse was white with alternating pink and blue pastel stripes, although the colors were graying from repeated washings. This was the outfit she wore as she climbed aboard the bus and headed toward Davenport. Her clothes looked a lot better back then, she said.

It took nearly three hours to get to Pittsburgh, where they stopped and idled in the depot for about 45 minutes. She did not get off the bus. They stopped twice on the highway in Ohio and once more in Indiana, but she remained in her seat, guarding her suitcase.

"I tell you, I've never done so much thinking in my entire life as I did on that bus, looking through the window, reading the neon signs and watching the headlights from the cars. Most of the people around me were sleeping, and none of them were too friendly. Not that I tried to do much talking. To tell the truth, I was scared half to death."

She wasn't actually thinking, she explained, as much as she was dreaming—with her eyes open. Her window was like an imaginary TV screen, and she could see the images of her past reflected before her. She saw her father carrying the cardboard box down to the side of the road. As the cancer took its toll, he had shriveled up like an old root. Then she saw the man who was to be her husband pull up. He put the cardboard box into the bed of the truck, opened up the passenger door, and helped her inside.

"I remember looking right into his face as he done this, the first time I had ever looked him full in the face. And then, as I sat in the darkness on that bus, I pictured how he looked earlier that morning when he leaned across the table and told me he was going to take away my teeth. And you know what? He was the same. Those 30 years we had spent together had bloated me like a balloon and wrecked up my face but, except for a little more gray in his whiskers, that bastard ain't changed one bit."

She paused, shook her head, chuckled, then shook her head again and again. It wasn't easy to suddenly accept the reality of what had happened. The shiny sadness of her life reflected in her eyes.

I looked away, down behind the tarpaper shack toward the outhouse across the field. It had a three-hole bench. There were four or five old cars dumped into a gully behind the outhouse and an abandoned windowless schoolbus, teetering on the edge.

"I never made it to Davenport," she said, after a while. "But I got all the way to Chicago. You ever been to the bus station in Chicago? More people there than I ever seen, all in one place. Half of them don't speak English, and none of them was white. The moment I got off that bus, seeing all them colored and hearing all that foreign commotion, I was completely confused. I was hungry, but didn't want to spend any money. I also wanted to clean up a little, but with all them people, I was afraid to make a decision."

After a while, she found herself a bench back in the corner, out of the way, and sat down to try to think things out. She still had her ticket to Davenport, Iowa, but didn't particularly want to go there any more. She didn't want to go anywhere, as a matter of fact. She wasn't willing to move one inch from where she was. She must have dozed off, for the next thing she remembered was feeling a hand on her shoulder, shaking her gently. Someone was saying her name. No one would know her name in Chicago, so maybe she really was back home, about to emerge from a terrible dream.

But when she finally opened her eyes, an elderly man with horn-rimmed glasses and a tiny, pinched nose introduced himself as a representative of the Traveler's Aid Society, whatever that was. The man's voice was soft and reassuring. As he talked, he picked up her bag, wrapped his arm around her ample shoulders, helped her up, and led her across the bus station.

When her husband had discovered her missing, the man explained, he had contacted their minister, who somehow traced her to Pittsburgh, and subsequently to Chicago. There was also a Traveler's Aid representative waiting at the Davenport bus station, just in case she had made it that far.

They were moving at a brisk pace, passing the ticket counters and neatly wending their way through the milling crowd. She felt like a piece of livestock. "Where are you taking me?"

"There's a bus to Pittsburgh leaving in about ten minutes. Your husband already wired the money." He smiled and continued to talk to her in his quiet and reassuring manner, as they pushed through a big set of swinging doors and headed on down a broad cement runway towards a long line of idling buses. Drivers in neatly pressed gray uniforms stood by the doors of their respective vehicles puffing cigarettes and punching tickets, as she and the man hurried by.

"But I already have a ticket to Davenport, Iowa."

"You can cash it in when you get back home . . ." He paused, all the while continuing to lead her down along the row of buses. "Of course, I can't force you to do anything you don't want to do." He shrugged and smiled apologetically. "I can't even help you make up your mind."

By this time, they were approaching the bus to Pittsburgh. She felt his hand on her back, urging her gently toward the bus. He handed a ticket and her suitcase to the driver.

Meanwhile, she hesitated, momentarily resisting the pressure on her back. She tried desperately to think things out, but her mind was blank, as was her future.

With nothing better to do, she walked up the steps, dropped into a seat by the window, and closed her eyes. She did not allow herself to open her eyes until hours later, when the bus pulled into Pittsburgh. She was so confused and embarrassed, she had completely forgotten to say good-bye to the man with the horn-rimmed glasses who had helped her.

Now she looked up at me, smiling and winking. "My husband came to meet me." The thought evidently amused her, for she shook her head back and forth, chuckling. "On the way home, we talked things over, got everything out in the open for the very first time. I told him how lonely I was, how it wasn't fair the way he constantly mistreated me. I said that I should be consulted in his decisions about how we spend our money. I told him that I didn't have enough clothes, that I wanted to go into town more often, and that, because he was such a damn hermit, I didn't have no friends or family." She nodded emphatically. "I let him have it with both barrels. He had never allowed no one to talk to him that way before in his entire life."

I stood up. More than two hours had passed since we had first started talking. The sky was clouding over. In this part of western Pennsylvania, rain erupts suddenly, swallowing the hillsides and ravaging the roads. Besides, I was getting cold, sitting so long on that stoop. And my pants were filthy, where the old coon dog had tracked mud all over me. I walked briskly back to my motorcycle.

"He tries to be nice," she said, as she followed along behind me. "But you really can't change him. You couldn't ever change my daddy either," she added. "When you come right down to it, they was both dark and silent men."

I nodded, pulled on my helmet and kicked down on the starter. The machine cranked to life as I straddled the seat. From past experience, I knew that I couldn't wait for the right moment to leave. Otherwise, I'd be waiting forever. I had to depart even while she was still in the act of talking.

She planted her foot in my path and grabbed my arm. "You know, he drove by two or three times while we was sitting here talking. He'll want to know who you are and everything was said. Hell," she said, smiling and winking, finally stepping out of the way, so that I could pull out, "I ain't telling him nothing. It serves him right."

The woman prepared herself extra special for her husband's homecoming that evening.

She went into the pump house and sponged herself down from head to toe, ran a brush through her hair a hundred times, scrubbed the grime from her fingers until the half-moons of her nails were white. Back in the house, in the loft where they slept, she got out the nice green cotton jumper dress with the pretty yellow and white floral design and laid it out on the quilt. He had bought her the dress the day she came home. She had only taken it out of the box once, the following Sunday when they went to church.

After preparing dinner and setting the table nice and neat, she went back upstairs and put on the dress. Then she dusted herself with some fancy-smelling powder she had ordered through a magazine and gotten in the mail. She was just about ready, when his truck crackled outside on the gravel. He walked into the house. She could hear him move about downstairs, looking into the big pot on the cast-iron stove, sniffing what was for dinner. But not until he walked across the room and started up the ladder toward the loft, did she reach into the water glass on the nightstand beside their bed. Only then did she put in her new teeth.

"A Garden in Winter"
BY JEANNE MARIE LASKAS*

This was supposed to be the weekend I put my garden to bed for winter—time to clip the lilac suckers, mulch some perennials and tuck in a few last bulbs—but instead I'm on a train to Philadelphia to say goodbye to a friend who is dying. I had planned for my hands to be happily immersed in dirt, but then I got the call asking, "Will you come hold my hand?" She never asked me to hold her hand before. I'm thinking about her, and my garden, and suddenly I'm reconfirming my resolve to specialize in perennials, plants that only pretend to die. They surprise you each spring with a resurrection you never really expect, but then there it is.

Some gardeners here in Zone 7 are engaged right now in the noble struggle to make winter gardens grow. I hear tales of plastic sheeting over spindly carrot plants and other extravagant ways to deny frost. Year-round gardening in Washington is possible, depending on what kind of gardener you are and what you're in it for. People grow spinach, lettuce, beets and cabbage all winter long. And leeks, you can always

*Published originally by The Washington Post Magazine, December 13, 1900. Reprinted with permission of the author.

count on leeks. To get these crops to grow you have to fuss with the aforementioned sheets of plastic and bales of straw, and corrugated cardboard, and drip irrigation systems, and all manner of complicated doohickeys one concocts to beat winter at its own game.

I am not one of those gardeners. For one thing, I don't grow vegetables, only flowers. Secondly, I enjoy the change of seasons too much to want to tussle with them and try to make them behave my way. Generally speaking, I have always found that it is more fun to ride the winds of change than it is to do battle with them. And anyway, I believe that the most delightful winter garden is the one you have in your head.

Winter is a time for thinking, planning, imagining how beautiful your yard will be next year, even though this year it may not have turned out so good. Winter is a gardener's holiest time, an opportunity to examine the stupid sins of last year's growing season and repent. Only in winter do you have time to read all those garden books you acquired with such lust over the summer. You can focus on the details of what any given plant was supposed to do, according to the books, and compare that information with your plant's less than exemplary life story. You try to store growing hints in your brain until next year so you'll be a better gardener, a smarter gardener, the greatest gardener in the world, perhaps, but usually you don't, and so you aren't, and deep down you know you never will be. Winter is a time to stare out the window at your barren plot and wonder why in the world you bother.

How did this garden become so important?

The window I'm looking out right now displays not my garden but a pumpkin patch whizzing by. The people sitting behind me on the train are talking about the old lady who fell off the train last year. She wasn't paying attention as she walked from car to car, to car to car, all the way to the back of the train, to the last car, to the last door, out of which she stepped and landed—plop—on the railroad bed. They didn't find her for two days. She didn't die, though. The people behind me are saying she must have been a crazy lady, or else drunk. I don't know why they aren't blaming the train, instead of the lady.

The lady I am going to visit is crazy, some people say. This makes me mad. She's hard to get along with, I guess, and can get ornery. She is 87 years old and fully in charge of her life. I have always liked visiting her because she can so quickly delight in how ridiculous and pathetic the world looks sometimes. Politicians make her laugh. Doctors make her laugh. Corporate America makes her laugh. She laughs at all that she refuses to believe in. Maybe this is the definition of crazy; I don't know.

She lives alone. She's taken care of herself, lived an adventurous life, and even in old age refuses to be cared for. She'd not seen a doctor or taken a drop of medicine in more than half a century. A week ago, at home, she had a stroke. She called an ambulance. She lasted a week in the hospital before she drove the doctors crazy enough to let her go home. The stroke took away control of her mouth and right eye and her ability to walk. They put one of those automatic beds in her dining room and a portable toilet next to it. And there she was left.

She tried to sleep in that bed. By midnight the first night she had climbed out of it. She got on her hands and knees and crawled up the steps to her old bed. She called me. Here she would sleep, she said. Here she would die, she said. That was when she asked me to come hold her hand.

I came into gardening the way all gardeners come: I took a path of utter ignorance. I knew next to nothing about plants when I bought my house and inherited this amazing yard. It's kind of an odd setup. My house sits at the end of a compact city street where there are no front yards. No yards at all, really, except mine, which runs along the side and back of my house, an L-shaped stretch of land that separates me from a railroad track. Freight trains come moseying by a few times a day. I have come to depend on the clatter, and I like waving to the engineers when I'm out there pulling weeds. Mine is an urban garden, a little oasis, a miniparadise surrounded by the noise and smells and warmth of the city.

As I said, I knew next to nothing about gardening when I moved here. And the truth is I didn't want to know much. I just wanted some pretty colors and sweet aromas to walk among. I looked at a few garden books and, like a lot of people, I suspect, I did exactly what the garden books said not to do. "Don't just go out to the local nursery and buy a bunch of plants," they all warn, in so many words. "You have to plan your garden. You have to think in terms of color patterns, basic groupings of line and form, harmony and accord, subtle balances of scale and proportion, mass and texture."

Yeah, yeah, texture smexture, I thought. I just wanted flowers. I went to my local nursery and discovered that flowers come in basically two types: the kind you only have to plant once because they come back every year, and the kind you have to keep planting over and over again because they die every year. Now, why would I want a plant that was just going to die on me, I reasoned, and so I stayed in the perennial section of the nursery. Next I discovered that perennials come in basically two types: the kind that bloom for a long time and the kind that bloom for a short time. Now, why would I want a plant that hardly ever blooms, I reasoned, and so all my garden decisions were made. I perused the nursery and read all the little tags attached to all the little plants and if it said "blooms all summer," I bought it. The only exception to this rule was if it was a plant I had heard of. These I also bought—lavender, baby's breath, daisies and other numbers on the gardening greatest hits list.

I took my garden home in my hatchback. No problem. It was as easy as buying a new set of dishes. I pulled each plant out of its pot and stuck it in the ground. I turned on the hose, looked up at the sun, said, "Go for it, guys," and felt happy. I would now have flowers, all summer long, for the rest of my life.

Well, you know the rest of the story. Some plants died immediately and some waited (politely) a few weeks before they died, and most stuff just sort of sat there and did nothing for the first year, and a few plants took over and grew so big and tall they smothered the smaller plants, and I couldn't remember what any of them were called, and I got really disgusted by all these rude bugs that came in and gnawed on my plants ("SLUGS!"), and then there were all those damn weeds—"Is that a weed, or is that a plant I want?"—that just cluttered up everything, and then it wouldn't rain enough, and then it would rain too much, and by September of the first year I was suffering from a fairly profound depression.

The heck with this, I said.

How I got from this point to my present delightful obsession with all things that grow in a garden—perennials as well as annuals and shrubs and weeds and beetles—is a mystery gardeners throughout the ages have likewise pondered, I suspect. I believe the earth continues to call you, once you get your hands in it.

A garden is a relationship. You wouldn't have started it if you knew what you were getting yourself into: something difficult and messy and maintenance intensive. Still, it fills up empty spots you never even knew you had inside you. You dig deeper and deeper into the earth and the joy you take from your time on this planet becomes richer and more complicated and fuller than that of any dimension your mind could have invented.

My relationship with my 87-year-old friend began about 10 years ago. I was writing a series of stories about old ladies and she was the most intriguing of all, a balloonist who spent her life breaking world records up in the sky. She was a wildly eccentric character who loved flying—almost as much as she loved cutting the grass. Often when I'd visit she'd be just climbing down off a gigantic farm tractor, proudly displaying the grass runway she had just mowed smooth. She did this for her husband, a pilot who would land his airplane there. She did this for him for years after he had died, as if expecting him to zoom out of heaven and come back in for a landing at any moment. A lot of people said she was crazy for doing that, but she didn't care, and neither did I. Often she and I would get in her car and drive down the runway, just for fun. "See how smooth it is, dear! Velvety smooth!" Other than that we would just eat lunch, talk, maybe go to the bakery or explore the fields of wild flowers. My visits became more frequent over the years as the bond between us grew tighter, and although we loved each other, I can't say we ever got to know each other very well at all.

I feel a similar way about my flowers. I mean I don't know these things at all, not really. I don't understand them. I don't understand why some of them crawl into the earth in the winter and then reappear in the spring, and some of them just throw seeds and then give up living, and some of them propagate with cuttings, and some you have to break up every two years, and some just go along happily cloning themselves with underground tubers. How remarkable! I keep finding more and more plants I want to try, just to see how each has worked out this game of growing, propagating, and dying—the same game all of us are in, I guess.

My garden now is broken up into areas I think of as rooms, connected by hallways. The hallways are lined with day lilies and begonias and impatiens and easy stuff you can count on. Right outside the kitchen window is the living room. I have formal beds there, snapdragons, blue salvia and blankets of sweet alyssum—and lots of pots of geraniums edged with lobelia, like you see in Ireland. Up the hill and beyond the lilacs, sort of hidden away, is a big room I think of as the bedroom. It's kind of a private area, just for me, a reading space and a sipping-Diet-Coke space, and last year the clematis vine went wild up there and filled the place up like Eden. Next year I'm thinking: more clematis. Maybe some jackmanii this time, or montana. And also morning glory. Flowering vines definitely inspire greed in me.

Way out in the front of my yard, by the picket fence, is the playroom. This is where the largest flower beds are and the place I try out new plants just for fun. This is my favorite room because this is where most of my perennials are, or at least where most of them were born before they got transplanted to other beds. Bleeding heart, red cloud spiderwort, edelweiss, columbine, bee balm, sea pink, salvia, silver mound, primrose, lavender, hosta by the ton, yarrow, lythrum, astilbe in many colors and heights—and countless others. My cat sleeps in a huge mat of coreopsis on summer's hottest days, and at night when I get home I have to comb it upward and help it stand up straight again. I'm quite bonded to that coreopsis, somehow, but then again so is my cat.

I don't really have a favorite plant. Like a good parent, I don't arrange love that way. My perennials do thrill me with their loyalty, though. I'll be snooping around in the garden in spring and there one of them will be, all supple and tender, rising up from the earth, seeming to yawn after some excellent hibernation. And my heart will leap up. "Hey!" I'll say, "Hello there!" right out loud. So begins a summer-long conversation.

My mind is wandering like crazy on this train. There's an Amish boy across the aisle from me, reading a book on horse breeding. In front of him is a boy his same age with a Walkman turned to maximum volume so we can all hear the tinny beat over the train's low rumble.

I'm thinking about that lady who fell off the train. I wonder what it would be like to fall through midair and be left alone like that—while everybody else just keeps on going, whizzing down the tracks—and there goes your luggage and everything else. Is that the feeling of death or is that just how we fear death will be? We get dumped somewhere and watch the world chug on without us, getting smaller and smaller until it disappears, nobody even noticing we fell off.

That's the fear, I suppose, but I don't think that's what death will be like at all. I don't think we'll care at all about the train that keeps on going without us.

When plants stop blooming, surely they don't miss their days of blooming, do they? Blooming is just a stage. The flower falls to the ground, returns to the earth, and becomes food for other plants. Where did we ever get the notion that the bloom was the only real thing, that everything before it and after it had to be defined in terms of it? What if the bloom, the life, were defined in terms of death? Then death would be the real thing and life would be just something you do in order to get there.

When the train finally pulls into 30th Street Station, I get a taxi, and when I arrive at my friend's house, I let myself in. I see the automatic bed in the dining room that she abandoned, and the toilet. "Hello?" I yell.

"Hello, dear," she says. "Up here." I go up into her bedroom, a place I was never allowed to enter before. It is very messy and very dusty. She is lying there, in a single bed, in the darkness of the late afternoon. I put the light on. "Look at that tree," she says, motioning toward the window where a tall oak stands. "Isn't it wonderful?"

"Wonderful," I say, thinking, this is it? This is how she's been amusing herself? Not with some TV show—well, she's never owned a TV—not with her beloved Larry King, whom she would never miss on the radio; not with the books that were once her passion. She just wanted to watch the oak tree.

"My feet are freezing," she says. "Would you fix the blankets?"

I go over and smooth them out around her feet and then tuck in her shoulders too.

"You're good at this," she says. "Have you been tucking in a lot of dying old ladies?"

"No, you're my first," I say. We laugh. She reaches out for my hand and I give it to her. Her skin is surprisingly soft. How do old people get baby's skin? I wonder.

"Guess what," she says. "I've decided not to die."

"That's good," I say.

"I'll die when I'm good and ready," she says.

"Would you like some soup?" I ask.

"Yes, dear," she says. "Let's have a picnic right here."

I bring up the bed tray with two bowls of soup and some bread and coffee, and I'm pleased to see her appetite is so large. But she is clumsy and has trouble feeding herself. The soup spills down her front. She is wilting. I face this. Night is falling and she asks me to turn on the outside light, which just happens to throw a spot on the oak tree.

"Isn't that wonderful?" she asks.

"Wonderful," I say, adding, "You want me to bring up the radio or something? Or why don't you try and read?"

"Oh, no," she says. "I have to watch the tree."

"All right."

"What are you working on now?" she asks. "Are you writing something funny?"

"An essay about my garden in winter," I say. Something about death and resurrection, I tell her. Or something about how flowers leave you, eventually, just like friends. So why bother? Well, because that's just the way it works.

"That's nice, dear," she says. "I love you too."

We say goodbye. It feels as if years go by before I finally make it back home to my garden, the tracks, the cat, my coreopsis crackling like brittle tumbleweed in the breeze. I get on my knees and cover the coreopsis with a blanket of shredded bark. I put the few last tulip bulbs in, a stately row of them between the picket fence and a patch of grape hyacinths due up in April.

It's good to stick your hands in the dirt sometimes. You can own the smallest plot of land in America and still it would be eight thousand miles deep. You start digging with your mind and pretty soon you're doing a free fall right through China. It's good to take a journey like that sometimes.

Thou Shalt Not Kill
MARGARET GIBSON*

The musical theme that opened "Boston Blackie" filled the living room. We heard hollow footsteps. Whistling. The silhouette of a man in a raincoat stepped into a dark city street, into a slick puddle of light from an overhead street lamp. He paused, turned his body toward us. A match flared. I saw his mustache and thick eyebrows. He lit his cigarette, the smoke curling over the brim of his hat. The man was a Yankee. Clearly, he was a murderer. I sat up straighter, chilled. But then came my mother and with a flick of her wrist she snuffed out Boston Blackie and all his matches, too evil for us to see. In 1956, I was 8, my sister 7. The television screen went gradually dark, with a diminishing blotch of light in the center. Then it was fully dark. I always believed I could smell smoke as I rocked back on my heels on the carpet, breathing more easily, released from the ritual of rapt expectation and disappointment that was my fear.

I knew my mother was afraid of strange men. I had seen her slyly put the hook on the screen door when a man she didn't know, a salesman with a suitcase of brushes and perfumes, rang the bell and stood on our porch. My sister and I should not open the door to any man nor speak to strangers on the street. Our allowed universe extended to the Stonewall Court, no further, unless we were invited onto Clark Road by a playmate, and to go there we had first to ask permission. Men stole children and sold them in gangs as white slaves. A woman's breasts had been sliced off by a man who had abducted her. When in hushed tones I told a friend my age about what had happened to this woman's breasts,

*Published originally in *Creative Nonfiction*, 2, "Poets Writing Prose," 1994. Reprinted with permission of the Creative Nonfiction Foundation.

she put both hands over her mouth and ran off laughing so hard I knew that she was terrified.

In Amelia County, away from the city of Richmond, my mother was more relaxed. Our Aunt T didn't have a television. In Amelia, everyone colored and white knew everyone else colored and white. But there were still snakes, black widows, the kicking end of horses, and broomstraw to look out for. Broomstraw? Broomstraw, my mother replied emphatically. A man who had been a neighbor, running across a field of it, had tripped and a stiff shaft of straw shot up his flared nostril, piercing the soft brain. He had been found on his face in the field. Aside from not being allowed in the barn without a grown-up, once out of Aunt T's house in Amelia we were turned loose to see whatever was there to see.

When Edwin killed a chicken, taking off its head with a hatchet, there was remarkably little blood. My mother was farm-bred. Killing hens for Sunday dinner was an ordinary occurrence, and neither she nor anyone else thought to warn us. Later I would know the signs of Saturday and its ritual slaughter. Marie wore her most faded print dress into the kitchen. After getting breakfast, she put a huge black kettle of water for plucking on to boil. The temperature in the kitchen already near 90, at not even 10 o'clock.

Sometimes she wanted her extra pay for Sunday dinner, a quarter, ahead of time. Aunt T grumbled but out came the quarter from her change purse and into Marie's grip. To keep it out of sight, out of mind, Marie put it on top of the can of pork and beans on the second shelf. "Miss T, she got Sunday dinner. I got Saturday night to think about."

We slipped away from the breakfast table and ran askelter through the kitchen. Marie was boiling water, paying us no mind. We banged out the back screen door, making as much noise as our bare feet could, slapping them down on the wood stairs. We were free until lunch. I wanted to go to the wooden house where Aunt T kept the new broods of baby chicks. I was shy of hens. When I was given corn to broadcast onto the dirt yard for them, I didn't cast it broadly enough. Or I forgot to be careful of my bare feet and wandered around in the feed area fascinated by the lidless yellow eyes of the hens, the fierce and accurate bobbing of their necks after glints of corn, the flounce of burnished tail feathers, and the manner in which each yellow foot lifted itself, flexed its nibbled toes, spread them out, and set them carefully down in slow motion while the fury of the bobbing necks kept up their rapt staccato. The hens were as intent as I was neglectful. Why then was I surprised, each time surprised, when the hard beak found its way to my bare toes, or fell between them in a near miss that teased me with delicious terror? I might have seen it coming.

To get to the house of the baby chicks, to be in that safe muddle of soft cheeping and down, puffs that could easily have been animated dandelions, we had to cross in front of the woodshed and continue on behind it. But on this one Saturday morning, I saw Edwin in front of the open shed, in baggy overalls, no shirt on. He was Marie's husband. A hen fluttered and squawked in one of his hands. He had her by the ankle part of her legs, and her yellow feet stuck out the back of a hand as big as a baseball mitt. Sun flashed off the head of the hatchet that hung in the ring of his overalls. I stopped still and watched him intently. What was he doing? He was whistling.

My sister—Betsy, we called her then—was lingering at the old bathtub set out in the yard. Although we weren't supposed to, she was running water into it from the old hose, raising the water in it to give to the cows and horses we always hoped would one day materialize from the pages of our books or from the pastures of more affluent farms in Amelia. She liked to sprinkle water on her toes and on to her exposed tummy soft and pale between the little ruffled halter and the elastic band of her shorts.

I turned back to Edwin. He didn't let on that he saw us, but then he never did. Why should he have to deal with Miss Doyle's city girls? I didn't know anything about his life, except that he was married to Marie, came to Aunt T's to chop wood, and he kept to himself. Years later, Marie would tell me he liked a beer on Saturday night. They had a boy named Junior who had been hurt in the war. He had one arm and pinned the empty sleeve of his shirt to the side of the shirt so it wouldn't flap. That's what Marie said he did when I asked her what about the empty shirt sleeve. I had never seen Junior. You could ask Marie questions, and she would answer in her sharp, high, amused voice. She gave me little jobs in the kitchen, swatting flies when they got too bad, and she let me pat the rolls into place on the tin sheets before she put them in the oven. Marie, my mother said, had a lot of white blood in her. That's why her skin was so nearly white. Edwin had darker skin, and he was quiet. It wouldn't have occurred to me to ask him a question, although I now wanted to. How burly the mitt of his hand was around the handle of the hatchet! How the sun lit the steel! And how was it that the hen, only moments before a flap and squawk of feathers, was now grown quiet, stilled perhaps by Edwin's gait, by a stride that rolled as if he knew the earth were roundly curved beneath his feet, a stolid rocking along the ground that had taken him now to the stump of cut wood. Barely breathing, I let myself be drawn to the wood stump, nearing it with my body, going away from it with my mind, wondering if I could get close enough to see the annular rings and know how old the tree had been when it was cut down. I must have known what Edwin was about to do.

In a motion so swift it was seamless, like light, came down naked arm, steel edge, and the weight of Edwin's determination to give Aunt T what she'd asked for Sunday dinner. And these powerful forces met in the neck of the hen, which I knew from sucking one cooked in Brunswick stew was an intricately interlocked lace of bones, delicate. Through feather and bone the hatchet fell, lodging into the surface of the wood with its orbiting years. The hen's head went over soundlessly into the wood dust and pine chips at the base of the chopping block. The eye was yellow with a jet black center, the beak hard and bright.

Next to me Betsy was an explosion of giggles, pointing for there in the dust, released from Edwin's grasp, the chicken, headless, ran its body in swooping arcs about the ground in front of the wood shed, looking for its head. Wasn't it looking? It was blindly, accurately looking. It did not bump into the stump or into Edwin's legs. He watched the swooping hen without expression. "It dancing," he said flatly. Dancing? The word astonished me. The body careened about the yard. Would it stop? Would it ever stop? Just then, it slumped to its side, near its lopped off head. I inched nearer the stump. On the rim of the blade, on the cutting edge, there was a faint blur I could call blood. Then I saw two bright drops on the wood rings.

"Do another one!" my sister demanded. She was delighted with the dancing dead hen. Appalled, I would never have asked although I was glad she had. I wanted to know if the frantic searching Edwin called dancing was what any chicken, headless, dead without knowing it, alive from the neck down, did.

"Miss T want two more hens for company Sunday," Edwin said.

He wouldn't let us think he was to kill another just because two white girls from the city, who didn't know what they were looking at, the difference between life and death, had asked him to.

Marie plucked the hens in a large bucket into which she had poured water as hot as her hands could stand. I wondered if her palms were pinker than the tops of her hands and fingers because they were faded by the scald of hot water. I shook off the idea. Were that so, her hands would be entirely pink. Edwin's hands were light and dark in the same way and so were the soles of their feet. There were things no one could explain, and color was one of them. A boy in school had a rosy stain that spilled across one side of his face, a birthmark. My grandmother the palest woman I knew, had splotches of brown on her hands, on her bosom and one dark patch on her cheek that had drifted up to the surface mysteriously one year and stayed.

Marie sat on a stool, knees spread, the bucket between her legs, hunched over. The burnished red feathers turned dark brown in the hot water. The yellow chicken feet turned yellower. Marie loved to suck the feet once they were cooked. She said they were "sweet." I worried about the toenails and never asked for a suck of one. Nor did she offer. Sometimes Aunt T let Marie take a whole hen home for herself, but most of the time the hens stayed on the Harvie yard or on the Harvie table. "The feets is mine," Marie said, and she could have them sticking up like broken witches' umbrellas, evil angles with small curved spurs. I hated the smell of blood and hot water and wet feathers. Sweat kerneled on Marie's forehead and slid down her neck into her dress, where it darkened the area around the collar and shoulders. The feathers came out more easily in the hot water. Marie grunted softly as she yanked at them. I thought she had forgotten that I was there. Then she looked at me sharply. "Law, child you gonna faint?"

Aunt T had smelling salts in her purse. I had gone into her purse on the sly to sniff them. She wouldn't allow the salts uncapped unless someone were light in the head. "They're powerful," she had said, "but each sniff takes the power off." The salts turned out to be horrid things that made my nose prickle and tears sting my eyes, a kind of punishment for being devious. Although now I was in fact light in the head, I didn't want Marie to fetch Aunt T and her salts, so I decided to duck out of the smell of water and feathers and blood, just as Marie said, "Run along now so's I can get these hens done before it gets any hotter." That was lucky. It appeared that I was minding her, but I was doing what I wanted to do. And I wanted the day to be hot, a scorcher. If the day were a scorcher, Aunt T would let Betsy and me fill the bathtub in the yard, and we'd go swimming. That is, we'd sit one at either end of the tub facing each other and hit the surface of the water to slosh each other in the face. Or we'd put the hose down inside the bottoms of our two-piece suits so that the water tickled and bubbled along the pale skin that never saw daylight, now that we were declared too old to run naked. In Richmond, even in the summers I kept on my undershirt or wore a ruffled halter. In Amelia, we ran barechested in and out of doors no one bothered to lock.

Whenever my mother spoke of meals in the country, either in the "olden" days or at Aunt T's, she used the word platters. There were platters of fried chicken, platters of corn on the cob fresh from the garden. Garden peas or limas, sliced beets, shelled black-eyed peas, mounds of mashed potatoes, or new potatoes cooked in their skins, quartered and bathed in butter. These came to the table steaming in bowls. But when my mother said platters, bowls and gravy boats were included in the largesse of the word. When she said platters I could sense her mouth watering, could smell the crispy, oily chicken. Marie served the food, bringing it to the table on platters once everyone was sitting down and the blessing mumbled. "Bless this food to our use and us to Thy service." The food was blessed because it helped us serve others. But Marie served the table, Otelia served the plates, and everyone else ate too much, even in the heat. "Loosen your belt," my mother sang out, an instruction that included unbuttoning the top button of my shorts if need be. I was encouraged to eat. I was skinny, my chin could be used to pick walnuts. I should eat. My father had a belly, Betsy was born chubby. My mother squeezed herself into her girdle and struggled with the hooks of her broad bras. Daddy helped her to hook up. The day before we were due to leave the country, I'd hear my mother's voice, high as a bluejay's shrill imitation of a field hawk, call "T." She meant her voice to carry from the kitchen, past the phone that rang two shorts and a long, and into the office where T did accounts. "T, let me have one of these chickens to take home to feed my girls." And T would have Marie pluck her a hen. Again the voice, nearer the time of our departure, would call out, "T," and a request would follow, this time for the snaps simmering with the hambone in the stew pot, "for my two girls." I hated snap beans cooked until their seams split and the beans turned a washed out, flaccid olive drab. But Aunt T promised a ham hock—Mom could cook up her own green beans.

In Richmond at home, dinner wasn't served on platters. Mom fixed our plates in the kitchen, and we brought them to the table. Meals in Richmond included fare I never saw at Aunt T's farm, and that was why I thought Aunt T was rich. At home Mom made ends meet with navy bean soup and soft Nolde's bread, spaghetti with crumbled hamburger, and the dreaded salmon cakes with their tiny circlets of bone and little slimes of skin lurking somewhere in the patty, no matter how long it was browned in the skillet or baked firm in a mask of white sauce. I knew that we didn't have much money because Daddy didn't make much. That was why he stayed in the Army reserves and went away for a week each summer. If we were stretched, how, I wondered, did Marie, who was poorer than anybody I knew except colored Annie who had 20 children and did Aunt T's washing and ironing, make ends meet? In Marie, who was stout, ends had visibly met. She liked her stoutness and patted herself on the belly like a drum, to let me hear what the hollow inside sounded like. I couldn't figure how Marie got stout. My father praised her pies, especially the lemon chess. But if he weren't careful, he could keep trimming away at the pie on the dinner table until I squirmed, knowing that Marie wouldn't have much of an extra piece, if any, to take home in a carefully folded napkin in her purse, along with the extra rolls.

Marie's house was down a red, deeply rutted clay road. The car jounced in the ruts and red dust filmed the windows, no matter how slowly Daddy drove the car. Marie's house looked as if it had slunk into place and hunkered down, a slouch of gray and black tar paper and planking with a screened porch in front that had bits of cotton or newspaper stuck in the tears in the screening so mosquitoes couldn't get in. Smoke came out the chimney even in summers Marie had a wood stove, too. She had a well out back, a kind of miracle down into which we peered fearlessly to see, after miles of thick stone, the glint of a coin at the bottom. We weren't allowed near it without a grown-up.

"Can I go to the well first? Please?" I asked Mom.

"May I," she replied. Then she said no. We had to stay in the car.

I didn't know why we were going to see Marie anyway, I thought as I slouched back grimly into the upholstered cushion of the Chevrolet. The car was packed for the trip home; my sister and I had struggled over who sat where in the back seat. There was a best side of the car, the side that passed the most animals in the fields. We counted animals on each side of the car. Whoever had the most, won. I could count higher than Betsy could and had the advantage, unless I sat on the side where the graveyards were. The rule was you lost all of the animals you'd counted whenever the car passed a graveyard on your side of the car. We knew where the fields with the most cows were. We knew where the grave-yards were. Just by picking the right or left side of the car, we knew at the beginning of the journey who would finish it triumphantly. Today, I was going to, unless the shadow of death had fallen dramatically across a field while we were staying at Aunt T's. I had the best side. Ready to win, impatient to start home, I whined silently to myself. We'd already said goodbye to Marie after the Sunday dinner which had taken too long because Aunt T sent the roast back because it was pink. We'd packed, but no one had been able to find the two cigar box banjos my father had made for us to play, twanging rubber bands as we sang the words we didn't know to "Oh Susannah," except for the refrain, which we sang loud enough for everyone in the house to hear. We wouldn't see Aunt T for a whole year. Home, the small brick house Mom called the "little red hen house," seemed far away. Counting the animals was just around the corner.

Mom and Dad went into Marie's house by the front screen door, after warning us not to go near the well. Since we didn't know why they were stopping to see Marie, we couldn't guess how long they'd be inside or judge the time we'd have to sneak to the well, lean over the rim, and get back to the car before they came out frowning. I was halfway through counting empty cans on Marie's back stoop, many of them Crisco cans, when my father came out with his hat tipped back on his head, grinning. He had a large, rectangular wood and wire box in his hand. On the box a door flapped open. "Come on," he called, heading back of Marie's house, past the well, into the feathery green pine and scrub hardwoods.

Marie had rabbits! Marie had millions of rabbits—nearly 20. White, brown and gray rabbits, black ones, and some with mottled brown and white fur. We could each choose a rabbit, whichever one we wanted, and they were going home to live in hutches Daddy would build, he said, out back in the stand of three dogwoods, at the edge of the backyard near our play house. No, we could not hold them in our laps on the way home. Yes, we could put the pen at our feet and pet them. We both chose white rabbits.

The rabbits would not fly away over Miss Conrad's crepe myrtle and apple trees as had the bantam chickens we'd brought home after last summer's visit. We had been told they'd flown away. I wasn't so sure. I had heard dogs in the yard before dawn and their growling haunted me. Would the rabbits tempt neighborhood dogs? Our dog Rusty had been hit by a car and had died under our mother's bed. But now we had two white rabbits.

In building the first rabbit hutch and placing it on wooden legs high off the ground, my father was like Noah making an ark for animals two by two. The hutch was not lifted up and set high because we expected flood water from the James, but because rabbits that lived on bare ground might sicken and die. The bottom of the hutch was wire with square holes the size of the checks in a gingham blouse I wore. The holes were small enough so that the rabbits had secure footing, large enough so that their tidy, admirable pebbles of dung dropped through to the ground. From there my father would shovel the droppings onto the flower beds to feed the bulbs. My father was happy with his hammer and saw. And I was happy thinking how much better off our two rabbits would be than those who lived on the earth, barren or grassy. My mother had told me stories of cutting the barley or wheat fields on her childhood farm. The mower went round the border of the fields, winding in and in toward center, driving the rabbits to a core of standing grain. Then the mower would be shut off, and in the quiet of circling hawks, the farm hands would take their rifles and go into the stand of grain to shoot the rabbits that had huddled there, clear of the rackety menace of the mower. I was glad that we had been able to make for our rabbits a refuge, an ark.

I named my rabbit Peter. Betsy named hers Snowball. We named them without knowledge of their genders, nor were we encouraged to peer into the posterior privacy beneath their puffs of tail. Soon enough there were six rabbits. Then eleven. Then twenty. Too many to name. But how serene the original Snowball rabbit was. She could sit unmoved for as long as I could remain quietly watching her, only her fine quirky nose twitching like the winter shivers. I suspected that the nose was connected directly to the heart of the rabbit, which I had felt thump with a terrifying rapidity when I held her up once by her chest to measure how tall she'd be if she stood up like the bunnies in the Easter books. I was as frightened as she was, breaking the rule that we were not to take the rabbits out of their cages. Didn't we remember what had happened to the bantam hens?

Peter and Snowball produced rabbits that were brown and gray and white or a mix of those colors, and they huddled together in the hay we stuffed into their hutches in the winter. The more there were, the warmer, especially the little ones which tumbled over each other and slept pell-mell with their paws and tails on top of other rabbits' heads as they burrowed into each other's fur. They were like my sister and me in bed with Mother and Daddy on the Saturday mornings that were made more leisurely by our not having to go to school or Sunday school at St. Giles.

After church on Sundays, our family came home and got quickly out of our good clothes. Betsy and I shrugged ours off, silk socks to the floor of the closet, patent leather shoes back in their boxes, our dresses and coats hung on hangers. My mother audibly sighed out of her clothes, the flesh pent inside her girdle gratefully released as she unzipped it at the side. Then she leaned over to unpin the hosiery from their little tabs and wire hooks, so that the soft brown nylon fell to her ankles. She'd flip off her high heels and then carefully, so not to run the expensive nylons, uncover her feet. Next the girdle. She'd scoot it off her hips to thigh level, a final tug, and down it would come. Flesh the girdle hadn't been able to tuck behind its elastic grip, and which had ridden up into rolls between girdle and brassiere, would come melting down. These rolls—she called them jelly rolls—were what Marie's turnovers turned into.

Before church, Mom put into the oven a pot roast or she baked a hen in a dented roasting pan that had a snug lid. She loved softbread, meat that was fork tender and fell off the bone, potatoes that steamed open and crumbled with the gentlest pressure of a fork. I was given white meat, my sister dark, her preferred piece a drumstick. Mother took breast and thigh, leaving my father with a leg, the back, the wings and the Pope's Nose, the last part of the chicken over the fence. It was a triangular plump piece that resembled the nose of a boy I knew after he'd fallen smack on his face in the playground. I nibbled the Pope's Nose shyly, once—just once. It was fatty, I spat it out. But the fat, my father said, was what made it sweet.

We hadn't had pot roast for what seemed a long time. Never mind sirloin. Steak was a sale at the Safeway or special occasion, like my birthday. For an eternity of Sundays we'd had chicken baked, chicken fried, chicken in lumps in a cream sauce on rice. One Sunday night when we were playing cards, only a half an hour from bed time, Mother drew a card from the pile after Betsy sniggered "Go fish!" She fanned out the cards in her hand and said, "You know, Marie and Edwin wouldn't do as well as they do without their rabbits." I thought about Marie's house, smaller than ours. What did "doing well" mean for Marie and Edwin? They were colored, and the country seemed far away from us in Richmond, where the only colored I saw regularly were women waiting for buses in the afternoon on Grove Avenue, or the maids in white uniforms pushing strollers around the block. "They'd be a lot hungrier if it weren't for Aunt T's goodness to them, and their rabbits." Suddenly I understood. Rabbits were how Marie got stout and made ends meet. From the depths of this insight, I heard her say that rabbit tasted a lot like chicken. I shivered, suddenly afraid that there was something I shouldn't ask. My father, I noticed, was frowning. We finished the card game and said the prayers that gave our souls into safety for the night and then we slept.

On the next Saturday we drove with our parents to the egg farm out Tllrec Chopt Road. This farm was the nearest thing in Richmond to Aunt T's farm, a white frame house that needed painting, a dirt road that raised clouds of dust behind the car, and a half dozen tumbled down outbuildings here and there behind the big house. Mom bought her eggs here because they were brown and fresh from the oven of the hen's body. Brown eggs tasted country. This Saturday she bought extra eggs for the meringue she would make for a special pie on Sunday. I begged for chocolate, overriding my father's plea for lemon. "Chocolate it is," she promised.

That Sunday we were allowed to eat dinner in our shorts. Early April was warm and Betsy had already been up to something in the backyard. She had plans for a new hideout underneath Miss Week's tree that wasn't a willow but drooped over like one and made a dark tent inside. In the shade of this nameless tree, she planned to spend Sunday afternoon, letting me in only if I knew the password. Since Saturday night she'd been taunting me with the need to know what the password might be. I pretended not to care. I was above passwords, she could hide out all she pleased. Dinner came to the table on plates prepared in the kitchen. The chocolate pie with perky peaks of meringue was sitting on the stove like a kept promise. I took in the glasses for milk and sat down. On my plate was a mound of potatoes hollowed out, with a well of gravy in the center. Also corn niblets from the can with the green man on the label. And chicken.

My piece of breast meat looked queer. Instead of the crispy tapered end where I usually found the soft fold of cartilage that held the tenderest meat, this breast was blunt at both ends. I turned it over to see if there were the ribs I liked to suck, but Daddy said not to play with the food. He was about to say the blessing.

After his voice had stopped rumbling over the words we knew too well to listen to, I looked around to see if it was OK to poke my fork into the chicken. Perhaps it was a thigh. I would have to eat the dark meat and watch out for the thready vein that reminded me of blood.

Chickens didn't fly, that's why the white meat was tenderest. White meat was lazy, dark was used muscle—in fact, the last muscle the hens used, dancing about without their heads.

Suddenly my sister's face turned red and splotchy. Tears spurted from her eyes and splashed off her chin missing her cheeks altogether. "Snowball," she cried, pushing her plate into the middle of the table. In the middle of the table was a large white Wedgwood bowl I liked because two rams' heads faced off in opposite directions. Inside it my mother put a clever disk with sharp needles. She called it a frog, but it didn't look like a frog. She had daffodils stuck into the tines, and these nodded out of the ram's head bowl, nodding in assent, agreeing with my sister's allegation and outraged grief. Her lower lip trembled. She looked at our father with a lowered brow that would butt like a goat's at anything in her way. Tears streaked her face now. My father's eyes met my mother's, smack over the daffodils.

"I can't eat Snowball," I murmured and put down my fork. I felt pale and cold. I had been about to eat, and I knew it. I remembered the rule: Eat what you're served. But Betsy had known what I'd only been on the brink of knowing. Not quite knowing, obedient, I would certainly have eaten the mother of all the little bunnies in our ark.

Mother pushed back a wild frizzle of gray hair and began to explain that we had to eat, money was tight just now . . . but my father interrupted. He said her name. Would he look at her the way he looked at her the night before he took me down to the basement for a strapping? I knew without looking that his eyes never left hers as he said to my sister, "Don't cry, honey, just eat the potatoes and corn and forget the rest."

After lunch, I ran out the back door into the yard to check the hutches. Peter was there. Several smaller bunnies were nibbling on greens. That meant Betsy had snuck carrots and lettuce out of the icebox and taken them down before lunch. Snowball was nowhere to be seen. As suddenly as Betsy had known what the chicken that wasn't chicken was, I knew her secret password. The word that had served to taunt my ignorance. The word that had been her tease of power over me all morning before church. The word no one in the family now would utter aloud. Snowball.

As for the rest of it—how Snowball got dead, whose ax, whether she danced in her blood and white fur—I forgot on purpose to think about these things. I forgot intently, and so thoroughly that now I can't remember if I, if anyone, spoke words of comfort to my sister, who went to her room and wouldn't come out, not even for chocolate pie.

I Give Up Smiling
BY DONALD MORRILL*

Before I went to live in Changchun, China, what I knew of thronged street life derived from a few gyrating days in Manhattan. On Garfield Avenue in my hometown of Des Moines, the only crowd—if it could be called that—gathered on 10 consecutive August nights, drawn by the first booms of fireworks that concluded the grandstand show at the State Fair nearby. Mostly mothers and children, we watched the colors spray and then droop into heavy mops of smoke over the poplar trees, the women talking in the quiet interludes between displays and for a few minutes after the finale, parting, at last, to put the younger children to bed.

Other than this—and a few porch sitters and occasional barbecuers—my best friends Sam and Lou and I were mostly the street life of the neighborhood. We delivered morning and evening newspapers, often camping out in each other's backyards in summer or mapping elaborate projects around the pot-bellied stove in our clubhouse converted from a gardener's shed. We lounged on the curb in front of Andy and Bill's Grocery, hungry for its racks of fruit pies and 16-ounce Cokes opened to us at 6 A.M. We bombed buses with snowballs and shot baskets in slushy twilights. We nursed soda fountain cocktails at Strait's Pharmacy, eager to be teased by our half-dozen idols who gathered there after their day shifts at factories, each of them coolly 21, getting laid and making

*Reprinted by permission of the Creative Nonfiction Foundation.

payments on cars that could put down rubber in four gears. Adventurers in smuggled six packs of warm beer, we knew in the dark the whereabouts of every clothesline and merciless watchdog for blocks in all directions.

The only other person with whom we truly shared the territory was Mrs. Whittenhall.

10.16.85, Changchun

Most mornings here, a young man in an olive greatcoat practices his trumpet. On the broad sidewalk in front of the main building, legions perform Tai Chi at dawn, and stooped ancients chat, hands folded behind their backs cradling a loud transistor radio.

Yesterday, the rationing of cabbages for winter began. Floods, I'm told, reduced this year's crop, yet most people can still afford to buy supplies beyond their government allotment. On corners around the city, people queue before green heaps, leaves splayed and twisting this way and that. Rumpled women in white cotton caps weigh each party's load, which is then strapped to the back fender of a bicycle or stacked on a push cart. Everywhere the chosen stalks lie side by side on the pavements and roofs and garden walls, the heart of each pointing in the same direction, a pale green root in pale autumn sunlight.

The women weigh all day long, though the wind stings cheeks and temperatures dip into the 50s. They wear white smocks and the customary five layers of underwear, standing in the street with hands on hips or sitting down with legs flat out, leaning with their tea against the cadre's wall next door. Their faces are worn but not brittle-looking like the women selling tofu in the street market, women who stand outside winter or summer, sounding more hoarse each day.

And then a young woman arrives—one of the new, fashionable women with long, curled hair and earrings dangling; she's outfitted in stubby-heeled shoes, black stretch-pants, the ubiquitous dull brown blazer (but taken in more daringly at the waist) and the equally ubiquitous black silk gloves, too thin to provide much warmth but elegant, sexy—and incongruous, gripping the handle of a cart empty but ready for greens.

Once in the morning, once in the evening, Mrs. Whittenhall walked the six blocks from her house on Dubuque Avenue to Andy and Bill's Grocery. She purchased a few items—a bar of soap, a loaf of bread—and always a large bottle of Pepsi, which she sipped on her walk back. For the neighborhood, this routine was as much a gauge of the hour as sunlight on leaves. Dependable, too, were her sweat-darkened, floral dresses, her slippers, and the windbreaker she wore only on the most frigid days. A blocky, ruddy woman with long, straight, graying hair, she always clutched a round, styrene plastic case in which you could see a swaddled Barbie doll—her child who had died years before, it was said.

My friends and I called her "Smiley," but it seems now that her unvarying expression was more of a wince stalled at its inception. She seemed always to be looking ahead, which made passing her on the sidewalk more excruciating. Once, without provocation, she said "Hi" to me. A soft, tight bleep, it shook and baffled me like a door in the night blowing shut.

She lived alone in a small white house nested in high weeds replete with butterflies. A man who said he was her husband once stopped me on the street to inquire about subscribing to the newspaper, but I never saw him again. When I passed her place on my paper route, I wondered what she did during all the hours she wasn't going to and from the store. I wondered what her house looked like inside. Someday I would have to find out.

We wandered into a restaurant a few blocks from the Chang-biashan Hotel and found ourselves opposite three round tables occupied by a wedding party. The bride and groom, probably in their 30s, were dressed in blue Mao suits. The bride wore earrings, and makeup, both of which suggested how plain she must usually look. On the back of the groom's head, a half-erect cowlick wagged. All through his and her hair multi-colored confetti glittered. Though only 11 a.m., he grinned a little wider from toasting with bai jiu (white spirits), and he insisted that Monica, Doug and I smoke with our lunch. We accepted the lights, though Doug has taken three puffs in his life, and I'm still nursing a burned epiglottis. Another man about his own age kept sweeping the groom away from our table with the arm-around-the-shoulder technique. I kept watching the bride, who would have seemed homelier had the groom been more handsome. Traditionally, the daughter-in-law occupied the most tenuous position in the family—subordinate to husband, father and older women. Unless she came with a dowry, she was an extra occupier of space and a belly, and had to earn her way doubly. She sat at the end of the table with the other women and all the children.

We finished our meal with only a few more interruptions. Another drunken reveler showed Doug how to use chopsticks to eat the large biscuit Doug had been holding in his hand. Certain foods are too large to manage with chopsticks, this biscuit among them. Doug listened as the man held the biscuit gracefully betwixt the sticks. To eat with the hands, say the Chinese, is vulgar. When one sees the state of most hands here, one must agree.

Later, on the restaurant doorstep, Monica found the red ribbon worn by the groom. Heading the list of embossed characters on it was the sign for "double happiness." Monica decided to save it, a little bit of life in a stranger's pocket.

We backtracked to the compound along the trolley lines, the bar that connects the trolleys to the hot wire above sometimes flashing, the trolley's horns piping at intersections with the pitch and timbre of an empty quart bottle. Doug said that the cobblestones and the chilly, wet weather (the second wet day in six weeks) reminded him of his days in Berlin and the Italian woman there he had to keep away from.

Remembering the regularity with which I saw Mrs. Whittenhall, I wonder how much I really see now of my five-minute commute to and from work along Bayshore Boulevard in Tampa, where I live now. One of my friends declares that a few weeks of driving the same streets to the office and she feels "wildly trapped" by the repetition. She then changes her route. But why should a known way, a routine way, be any less new and full of possibility than a path on which one has never ventured? I like to believe that imagination nudges repetition into gratifying deviations. I like to believe that when I notice Hillsborough Bay is a powdery brown tipped with silver—like the color of mink fur—I've recognized the constant change, the inimitable condition of each moment among our shifting continents. Of course, this strategy aims for the same state of expanding potential, of collectable experience, that my friend craves when hysterical. It's only another wish to be immortal.

One of the beauties of sojourning is that in just walking to the post office and back, day after day, one can feel how fleeting things are, and are not. In Changchun, I could see a man on a street corner holding a chest X-ray toward the sun, a large pentagon shadowing the left lung. I could see a boy, alone on a soccer field at dusk, kicking a ball through eight inches of fresh snow. I could see a woman wearing a sweater with the word *hovering* woven across its front. Though I often roamed Changchun for hours, I just as often followed the same paths. Perhaps this gave me the same comfort Mrs. Whittenhall took from her walks. It echoed those pleasurable family trips down Highway 5 from Des Moines to Pershing, Iowa, my mother's hometown. Highway 5—that road I knew best as a child.

It was always late spring or full summer on Highway 5 because our family went to Pershing on Memorial Day, the 4th of July, and for an occasional reunion picnic. A two-lane road through corn fields, it was uneventfully straight except for several hills and dips—and a few sudden, pinched curves that elicited from my father a repeated diatribe on dangerous attempts to pass farm vehicles and the sadism of highway planners. A passenger, I could stare out the side window at the power lines rising and falling hypnotically as we passed pole after pole set along the shoulder. Cows and sheep and hogs in barnyards seemed still as statuary. A pollen-heavy haze hung over the crops, and the wind pulled my hair back flat and made such white noise that any remark from my parents in the front seat startled me.

The Chinese now welcome Japanese capital and technology, though a collective hatred burns under the surface, at least in this part of the country. We visited the provincial museum today specifically to view the wing devoted to maintaining the memory of Japanese atrocities during World War II. It's housed in the former palace of Pu Ye, the last Qing Emperor who was deposed and then made the puppet monarch of the Japanese-controlled state during the '30s. Young girls in white cotton dresses oversee each room of memorabilia, and through one of the windows we watched a man whack a horse in the belly repeatedly with a pipe because it couldn't pull the overloaded cart out of a rut. This was after he'd whipped it and then pounded its flanks with a long, heavy-gauge wire. Inside, as I strolled past photos of severed heads dangling from spikes, and skeletons in mass graves, past models of detention camps and the diorama depicting a Japanese soldier breaking a peasant's leg with bricks, I could hear the cry of the Jews, "Never again!"

Cottonwoods—planted by the Japanese occupying Changchun during the

'30s—now broadcast their seeds, making the central part of town into a nauseatingly languid snow-scene. This "June snow" gathers in the gutters, and I saw a small boy pile it up and put a match to some fist-sized, gauzy pyres. The stuff is a curse now not only for the memories it brings. It so suffuses some avenues, you can hardly breathe without whisking the air. Many women wrap their hair in sheet nylon scarves, but the flakes still catch.

Changchun's life is in its trees. Its willows are beautiful but more well-known for their strength which is attributed to difficult winters. And its poplars, slim, straight, were planted after the decimation of nature during the Communists' various programs to modernize, trees planted because they are quick-growing, trees that are now young, like most of the population.

I believe I knew every tree and gas station along Highway 5. The electric power plant with green windows overlooking the Des Moines River; the Knoxville high school mascot—a black panther—painted on a yellow watertower; the Uncle Sam mailbox post at the head of a dirt road winding to a white farmhouse: Each thing I remember now seems a monument animated by desperate nostalgia. Highway 5 was a world dependent on our passing through for its orderliness—right and rhythmical, even in its contingencies.

For instance, no matter how agitated or uncommunicative the family might be, we nearly always came together—leaning up in our seats and looking forward—as the car glided down a long slope a few miles beyond Knoxville. At the bottom, a narrow, metal suspension bridge spanned a creek. Given the traffic, we wondered if we would be forced to pass an oncoming car or truck on that bridge. My father, however much he abused alcohol, refused even a drop if he was to have the family in the car, but he seemed harried by the vision that a drunk driver would kill us all. Perhaps it was that the driver would be like his veering, lesser self that made him especially vigilant at the narrow bridge. As a camper or tilt-cab semi approached and the gusts of the non-collision rocked our car, my mother's lined cheeks plumped into daubs of white shortening. She always exhaled quietly, packing away fear with a curt clearing of the throat.

Beyond the bridge, the road ascended a long slope bordered on both sides by woods uncharacteristically dense and large for championship farm country. Halfway up, no matter how hot the weather, we passed through a zone of utter, sweet coolness—always a forgiving shade. There, below the south side of the road, stretched a glade in which stood a sizable, shacky house propped on blocks and sided with fake-brick asphalt panels. A fern of smoke rose from its chimney, and a creek wound past its front porch—past the gravid clothesline and the chopping stump and the junk cars. We seemed to sail through this "cool spot," always marveling at its dependable grace. It made us agreeable; our hot weather subsided for a moment, and the narrow bridge lay behind. That is probably why we named the place and looked forward to it, and why it is symbolic to me of those unburdening places we come to with others. In those days, I imagined that the people who lived there were happy, that they had peace, if nothing else. At the top of the slope—as the road flattened and the woods retired into distance—I sometimes would gaze unblinkingly into a cloudless sky until snake-like blotches seethed and whirled before my eyes, images that only I could see, that I believed were atoms.

Sun flickers through yellowing leaves. The flies have slowed down. An indistinct voice blares at the sports field two blocks away. In the street nearby, the junkman, seeking bottles, bangs his cymbals and yowls. Later, a man cranks an iron cylinder on a spit over hot coals until the temperature is just right; then with a bar, he pops open the end of the cylinder: BOOM! Basins of fluffy corn or rice blast into his mesh trap.

With three balls, three bowls and weary patter, a small, grubby boy performed tricks for a crowd in front of the No. 5 Department Store. A girl performed excruciating backbends. A boy wound a heavy-gauge wire tightly around her neck. In one motion, he wound it and she turned toward the crowd with her hands cupped, outstretched in supplication.

I asked an old man in front of the Changchun Restaurant to pose for a photo. With his cane, he pushed another old man—twice—out of what he determined would be the area within the picture. The other fellow, purple-red in the face, grinned—a single safety pin laced through his breast pocket and a white wicker basket full of scavenged beer cans. I took pictures of each.

In one, the pushed man stands with the white sun casting a metallic sheen on his eyelids—like eye shadow.

In the other, the shover grins, his teeth so many scattered nubs they look like blisters on his gums, his beard a triangular wisp that seems glued to his chin.

Were these their first photos alone, or at all?

Named after the World War I general called "BlackJack," Pershing lay at the end of an asphalt strip branching from Highway 5. Its grid of a dozen tromped-gravel streets still constitutes the remains of the somewhat larger company-owned mining town that flourished during the earlier decades of this century when, presumably, demand made it more profitable to burrow under the land for soft coal than to farm. Legend says our family started there in the late teens or early '20s when my grandfather, Albert Marshall, gave up a shot at pitching in the majors to marry my grandmother, Fay Cauldenburg, and work in the mines. The reason given for his choice is the same my father gives for exchanging his theatrical ambitions for a steady spot on the assembly line: He didn't like the travel and the being away from home.

Growing up, I often believed my father regretted his decision, that he felt he had betrayed his dream by forsaking it before it might have proved beyond him. My grandfather—who died just before I was born—appears to me in a single photograph, clad in a baseball uniform, the shade from the bill of his cap shadowing his eyes. Through my mother's reverent taciturnity, he speaks only in calm, patient tones, and I imagine her—a middle child of eight—loving him from her place among the faces. I once believed that because he and I were left-handed and I was her first born, I was her favorite child. He died of heart disease no doubt encouraged by the same coal dust that sometimes befogged Changchun like gaslit London. Perhaps his forsaken major-league prospect is a soothing substitute for talent, or possibility. I can only verify that my mother—who looks like her mother—could throw a baseball, and she taught me how.

Pershing could be roamed like the streets I shared with my three best friends and Mrs. Whittenhall. There, my cousins and I whipped Nazi commandos in Dracula Woods and careened at the steering wheels of cars rusting among weeds. On trampolines sunken like swimming pools in a lot called "Recreation Center," I bounced and romped until the glands in my throat ached. Using a ditch, I learned one day how to get on my cousin Jim's 26-inch bike—and rode and rode and rode, proudly waving at my relatives as I pedaled past on another town circuit, weary but perplexed as to how to get off the thing without injury.

During one family reunion, I watched men somehow get into the casual play of secretly passing around a twisted, muddy, bald baby doll. On finding it in his front seat or on his dashboard, each man would avenge himself by putting it on another man's hood or in his tacklebox, or in his cooler—where the latter would surely find it and pass it on, hoping to spy the next man when he discovered it.

That night, back home in Des Moines, my father found the doll as he unpacked the station wagon. He chuckled like a mother bewildered by a made-up game in which her children have included her. He took it into the house, and nothing more was said about it until one winter Sunday when he opened the sewing machine. He cleaned and straightened the doll's limbs and dressed it in a smock and bonnet fashioned from remnant satin. With rouge and mascara, he gave it back its eyes and the flush of infant health. He also transformed it in some other way I may never be able to articulate. Now, I see the doll as having suffered more than the men through whose hands it had passed, the doll as the unfortunate world into which we press our imaginings—another case of making too much of things.

In a box outfitted with supple white paper, my father sent the doll back to one of my uncles in Pershing—no return address, just a note pinned to its smock, "I've come back."

Pershing smelled of well water and blacktop. Its residents then, as now, went off to work at the VA in Knoxville, Rollscreen in Pella, or Maytag in Newton. Mustard jars and bread-wrappers and stacked plates cluttered its kitchen counters, and a sun-bleached plastic deer stood shyly in the yard. Pershing was my Aunt Myrna wet-nursing all of us kids—she had so much milk. It was vast husbands with deep bellybuttons recumbent in the shade, sipping Grain Belt beer and smoking Camels. Land of the double negative and the double entendre; of my cousin-in-law Walt plucking a string bass propped on a long, rubber-tipped screwdriver; of a fast-pitch softball team that in night games played rival towns: Attica, Bussey, Lovilia. Pershing was pride and formidable limitation, farm-pond fishing, and the dowdy gray stone my Uncle Tony broke open in his rock shed to reveal to me its glittering crystals.

Most of all, for almost two decades, Pershing also seemed a place of immortality. No one in our family there died, and few went away—until recent years.

I sometimes hear my fellow provincials wish aloud for more street life in their cities, for places where one could promenade, or linger safely, and regard the day or night abounding with strangers. The summer sunlight in Tampa—which can split dashboards and jab the brow like a searing spike—discourages outdoor cafes, though they are now coming into fashion in some quarters. The city has its joggers and dog-walkers and lunch-hour strollers, but like most North American towns—Des Moines included—the people who spend real time on its streets are mostly homeless, insane or for sale. Our only crowds near the size of street-market throngs in any provincial Chinese city gather for annual parades, sidewalk art festivals or musical beer bashes sponsored by local radio stations. Otherwise, we teem in enclosures.

Some years ago, in suburban New York state, I was dismayed to see parents shepherding their costumed children around shopping malls on Halloween, rather than around their neighborhoods, as was common when I was a child. For an ancient celebration acknowledging the darker spirits, these children dressed as cartoon versions of those monsters their parents took them to the mall to avoid. The treats dropped into their bags from the chain stores and anchor stores and food courts would contain no razor blades or poison, only positive community images, which is good for business.

Undoubtedly, this is one more sequestering from the immediate environment, one more exposure to the seamless display of the market. But then, what is the immediate environment? It was once common to refer to something that seemed wholly false as "plastic," as in, "This place is plastic." But isn't plastic just as much a real thing as any other thing? Isn't it "real" plastic? Only someone, I think, who is surrounded by too many goods rather than too few—someone not from Changchun—could see this as a crucial question.

Though the media in China never missed a chance to show disaster in the States, the Chinese I met who thought America a dangerous place pointed to the images the U.S. exports through popular film, which encourage visions of shootouts on every street corner, like gas stations and fast food. I also found a number of Europeans who wanted to believe in this violence, partly to stem their envy generated by the glamor of American publicity.

I am awakened occasionally by the newspaper's *plop!* on my porch at 3 AM, a newspaper now delivered by an adult in a car. I sometimes lie in that dreamy darkness before receding into sleep and remember how 25 years ago, I walked my summer route, smoking Swisher Sweets, majestically nocturnal and somehow feeling in charge of the landscape.

Two old men, near the Stalin monument, play checkers on the curb until midnight, several other men squatting around them and smoking cigarettes, looking on.

Barbells and guitar-strumming in a dim alley.

Lovers in a dark lane, one couple in each space between a row of lilac bushes.

Nearby, trunks of trees are whitewashed around their bases. "Socked trees," my father called them when I was a boy. "They are considered beautiful in China," he said, painting the elms in our back yard.

My neighborhood was safer then, I imagine, than now, but how much? Once, just after picking up my papers at the drop point on East 33rd Street, I noticed a distant figure backlit by the glow from Strait's Pharmacy. It approached at a stroll; then it spied me and started marching faster. No news-carrier bag hung over its shoulder, so I turned and began walking in the opposite direction. I glanced back. It was charging after me. I raced around the corner, my load banging wildly against my legs, and had just enough time to scramble among the bushes in Mrs. Gardner's dark back yard before the figure appeared and sauntered up Dubuque Avenue, fists at its sides, searching.

It was Wendell Wallace, one of the tree-service Wallaces from the semi-rural area beyond the end of my route. In Andy and Bill's lot at the close of a summer day, you could find Wendell and four or five of his grimy brothers draped on the bed of a tree-trimming truck, sipping Cokes, slit-eyed like cats facing a wind. He was 16 or 17 and had been in my eighth grade algebra class, intermittently, the year before. "Fuck" was the mortar of his speech, slapped between each block of three or four words. One time, he'd walked out of woods behind the softball diamonds at Stowe School, asking to join our pick-up game. Within minutes, he'd slugged Sam, one of my best friends, and was baiting Sam to retaliate, so he could hurt him. Sam, who grew up to be a platoon honor man in the Marines, was no coward, but he was no fool, either. He gave Wendell no eye contact and no excuse to do more. He knew Wendell liked to hobble dogs and hang kittens.

From the bushes—perhaps the only time I can honestly say I held my breath in fear—I watched Wendell pass. Recognizing me must have spurred his pursuit. Had he found me, I'm sure I would have learned something new about my will to survive. Who knows what fuel burned in Wendell?

I let him get far out of sight before emerging, and I waited until near daylight before finishing that part of my route near his turf. I never saw him again—which was fine—and several months later I heard that he'd blown his head off while cleaning a shotgun. The papers called it an accident.

In the years just after I left Iowa for good, I sentimentalized it as vigorously as I'd vilified it in order to leave. This response was like the mirthless grin we North Americans pony up for snapshots—believing as ever in packaging as content—not thinking that by this we forgo all the expressions that make up our faces for the meager record of a single gesture. I pinned that false smile on my neighborhood, on Highway 5, on Pershing and the rest—just as I affixed the nickname "Smiley" to Mrs. Whittenhall.

In China, I often found myself in public, smiling dumbly, reaching for the faith in universal gestures. I finally stopped. It seemed condescending to all that transpires between people, between our narrow bridges and our cool spots. I look back on the foreseeable routes and wayward wanderings of my sentences here and think of the palm-size notebooks in which I tried to "get everything down." Entries like *I walked with an anguished and ecstatic heart* and *Monica looked celestial, panicked* gain no accommodation under the obligatory smile. It imprisons our fairer history. Like our disposable horror at each day's headlines, it excuses us falsely from all we are and do.

Lee Gutkind

Lee Gutkind, founder and editor of the popular new journal *Creative Nonfiction*, has performed as a clown for Ringling Brothers, scrubbed with heart and liver transplant surgeons, traveled with a crew of National League baseball umpires, wandered the country on a motorcycle, and experienced psychotherapy with a distressed family—all as research for eight books and numerous profiles and essays. His award-winning *Many Sleepless Nights*, an inside chronicle of the world of organ transplantation, has been reprinted in Italian, Korean, and Japanese editions, while his most recent book, *Stuck in Time, The Tragedy of Childhood Mental Illness*, was featured on ABC's *Good Morning America*.

Former director of the writing program at the University of Pittsburgh and currently professor of English, Lee Gutkind has pioneered the teaching of creative nonfiction, conducting workshops and presenting readings throughout the United States. Also a novelist and filmmaker, Gutkind is editor of *The Creative Nonfiction Reader* (a series of anthologies, upcoming from Jeremy E. Tarcher–Putnam Publishing Group), and the Emerging Writers in Creative Nonfiction book series from Duquesne University Press. Lee Gutkind is also director of the Mid-Atlantic Creative Nonfiction Writers' Conference at Goucher College in Baltimore.